THE PASSEGGIATA AND POPULAR CULTURE
IN AN ITALIAN TOWN

The Passeggiata and Popular Culture in an Italian Town

Folklore and the Performance of Modernity

GIOVANNA P. DEL NEGRO

McGill-Queen's University Press
Montreal & Kingston · London · Ithaca

© McGill-Queen's University Press 2004
ISBN 0-7735-2722-2 (cloth)
ISBN 0-7735-2739-7 (paper)

Legal deposit first quarter 2004
Bibliothèque nationale du Québec

Printed in Canada on acid-free paper.

This book has been published with the help of a grant from the Canadian Federation for the Humanities and Social Sciences, through the Aid to Scholarly Publications Programme, using funds provided by the Social Sciences and Humanities Research Council of Canada.

McGill-Queen's University Press acknowledges the support of the Canada Council for the Arts for our publishing program. We also acknowledge the financial support of the Government of Canada through the Book Publishing Industry Development Program (BPIDP) for our publishing.

National Library of Canada Cataloguing in Publication

Del Negro, Giovanna P.
   The passeggiata and popular culture in an Italian town: folklore and the performance of modernity/Giovanna P. Del Negro.

   Includes bibliographical references and index.
   ISBN 0-7735-2722-2 (bnd)
   ISBN 0-7735-2739-7 (pbk)

   1. Sasso (Italy) – Social life and customs. 2. Plazas – Social aspects – Italy – Sasso. 3. Popular culture – Italy – Sasso. I. Title.

HN488.S27D44 2004   306   C2003-906894-3

Typeset in Palatino 10/12
by Caractéra inc., Quebec City

To my parents, my husband, and the people of Sasso

Contents

List of Figures

Acknowledgments

Throughout the various stages of this project I have been lucky enough to receive support and encouragement from a loving family, caring friends, stimulating colleagues, and nurturing mentors. I must of course begin by thanking my parents, Anna and Giovanni Fiore Del Negro, whose patience and affection have been unwavering, as well as my brothers, Osvaldo and Luciano, my sisters-in-law, Marlene Jennings and Marcelle Da-Meda, and my nieces, Tanya and Anne-Darla. I would also like to extend my appreciation to my in-laws, Judith and Charles Berger.

Over the years, the guidance, insight, and wisdom of Richard Bauman and Sandra Dolby have been invaluable to me. Their sound advice and generosity of spirit have always encouraged my intellectual creativity and interdisciplinary orientation, and for that I am deeply grateful. I am also indebted to John Bodnar and William Corsaro for sharing their knowledge and expertise with me. My exchanges with Linda Dégh, Marilyn Motz, Jack Santino, and Beverly Stoeltje have also stimulated my thinking about the study of expressive culture.

On trips to Italy I stayed with relatives, alternating between the home of my aunt Linda and that of my aunt Norina and uncle Michele. I cannot express in words the depth of their warmth, hospitality, and great kindness; my fieldwork would have been impossible without them. I wish to express my gratitude to the people of Sasso who shared their experiences with me and tolerated my endless questions. I would like to especially thank my cousin Massimo, who was

the best research participant a fieldworker could hope for. Our conversations informed almost every part of this study. I also benefited
from the help of ethnologist Adriana Gandolfi from *Il museo delle genti
d'Abruzzo* and Emiliano Giancristofaro, editor of *Rivista Abruzzese*.

I am grateful to my friends and colleagues in the United States,
Canada, and Italy for offering words of encouragement and advice
during the different phases of this book project. I would like to express
my deepest appreciation to John Ashton, Hande Birkalan, Eduardo
Bonilla-Silva, Umberto Bortolin, Mary Bucholtz, Kathleen Bickford,
Theresa Carilli, Anne Chin, Donnalee Dox, Cristina Fabretto, Emilia
Di Lullo, Mary Di Paola, Holly Everett, Kathy Ferrara, Sara Gatson,
Ghada Georgis, Heather Gert, Mary Hovsepian, Tazim Jamal, Joseph
Jewell, Tracy Kamerer, Kate Kelly, Jimmie Killingsworth, Patrick
Leary, Rosina Marchica, Howard Marchitello, Chris Menzel, Gloria
Nardini, Peter Narváez, Mary Ann O'Farrell, Arzu Öztürkmen, Franca
Pannese, Jim Rosenheim, Paola Russi, Paul Smith, Susan Stabile, Kati
Szego, Lynne Vallone, Igor Vojnavic, and Elizabeth Yeoman.

I would like to extend my thanks to Sabina Magliocco and Lola
Romanucci-Ross for reading and commenting upon earlier drafts of
the manuscript. I greatly benefited from their helpful criticism and
feedback. I am also grateful to the editors and staff at McGill-Queen's
University Press for their cheerful disposition and professionalism.
I want to thank Philip Cercone who invited me to submit my book
to the press and John E. Zucchi for his enthusiasm and commitment
to my work. A special thanks goes to editorial assistant extraordinaire
Joanne Pisano, who patiently answered all of my questions and
ushered this project through various stages of preparation in a timely
and efficient manner. For the help with the final manuscript, I also
wish to thank Leland Anderson, Joan McGilvray, Claude Lalumière,
and Cecilia Zucchi.

The financial assistance I received over the years helped to cover
various research related costs. Both the Richard Dorson Research
Award and the faculty fellowship from the Melbern G. Glasscock
Center for Humanities Research at Texas A&M University supported
field trips to Italy and allowed me more time for research and writing.
I am also grateful to my department head, Larry Mitchell, for a
semester faculty leave that enabled me to complete this project. This
book has been published with the help of a grant from the Canadian
Federation for the Humanities and Social Sciences, through the Aid
to Scholarly Publications Programme, using funds provided by the
Social Sciences and Humanities Research Council of Canada.

Support in a project likes this comes in many forms. Without the
wit of *This Hour Has 22 Minutes*, Canada's premier comedy show,

and the sounds of Lucienne Boyer, Petula Clark, Pino Daniele, Beau Dommage, Ivor Novello, and Michael Penn, this task would have been a much less pleasant experience. Periodic doses of *Law and Order* and *Six Feet Under* also provided me with an enjoyable respite from writing.

Finally, I offer my deepest gratitude to my husband and colleague Harris M. Berger, whose love, patience, and support made this undertaking significantly less daunting. The collaborative work we have done over the years has been enormously gratifying, and our continued conversations about the salient issues of our field continues to nourish my personal and intellectual life. His perspective on my work has always challenged me to think lucidly and creatively about my data and the broader theoretical implications of that material for social scientific and humanistic scholarship.

THE PASSEGGIATA AND POPULAR CULTURE
IN AN ITALIAN TOWN

1

"Our Little Paris"

Ma cosa è bella è il suo piccolo corso
tutti la sera d'obbligo il percorso vasche
annazie e arete comme'e nu fesso
è la passeggiata classica a Sasso

What is most wonderful is its little street
at night everybody dutifully on their path
back and forth like a fool
it is the classic passeggiata of Sasso.

Lino Venturi[1]

When I was a child, the stories my mother told me about Sasso, the small town in central Italy where she grew up, combined equal parts nostalgia, tragedy, and humor. My mother had a large repertoire of stories, and, though in my teens I began to tire of her didactic tales about the rural misadventures of her siblings and the hardships of the post–Second World War economy, I was always fascinated by her accounts of the passeggiata, the ritualized promenade so important to the town's culture. In these cinematic tales, I could rely on my mother to provide a cast of exotic European characters and a steady diet of local intrigue. Though complex squabbles over love, business, and local government were the meat and potatoes of these narratives, Sasso emerged in my mind very differently from *Peyton Place* – the archetypical home of mean-spirited and gossiping villagers that the mass media had implanted in the mental maps of my Anglophone friends in 1960s Montreal. No stodgy and colorless New England, the Sasso of my mother's narratives was a place where clothing and style mattered. In fact, it was through descriptions of dress, gait, comportment, and demeanor that these characterizations of passeggiata strollers were made. In her stories, powerful politicians were not just powerful politicians but elegant older men taking long and commanding strides in well-cut gray serge. Genteel gatekeepers of propriety, teachers were always depicted wearing tweed skirts and sweaters, always monitoring the piazza (town square) for inappropriate behavior in their students – present or past. Provocative teenagers overtly flirted with the opposite sex, and no sartorial detail, from the cut of a skirt to an ill mended hem, was ever left unreported. The costume shop of my mother's narrative mind was a busy place. More than this, my mother represented herself as a canny interpreter of social life. Critical commentary on the characters was frequent in these stories, and she made clear to her audience that she could always tell if a neighbor's messy crop of hair reflected an anti-social disinterest in appearance or the sudden loss of disposable income for a regular barber's visit. The terms may seem melodramatic, but so were my mother's tales. The passeggiata was, for me, a visual and theatrical place of wonder and endless possibilities.

If you ask the residents of Sasso about the town these days, more often than not the passeggiata is still the first thing they will mention. As a microcosm of village society, a battleground in the daily struggles of politics and gender, and fashion runway for displays of sophistication and style, the event is central to the local society. This book is a study of culture in Sasso with a particular emphasis on the passeggiata. It seeks to provide a rich ethnography of daily life in contemporary central Italy and explore a range of problems that center on the issue of modernity. In many ways, the Sasso that has emerged in the second half of the twentieth century is a quintessentially modern place. From the devastation of the Second World War, the town has seen the emergence of an industrial economy, the return of townsfolk who had earlier immigrated to foreign lands, the increasing presence of the mass media, and a transformation of gender roles. Though changes such as these are typically labeled by sociologists as "modern," this concept has undergone increasing scrutiny in recent years, and my study will show how social change is influenced by culture and the complex ways that people use expressive forms like the passeggiata to make such changes meaningful.

Though the town and all the people who live in it are real, the identities of the various participants in the project have been obscured; I have changed the name of the town to the fictitious term "Sasso" and refer to its residents as "Sassani." In the photographs, I have also blurred the faces of public figures and deleted the name of the town from the postcards.

The hilltop village of Sasso is located half an hour away from the Adriatic Sea and has a population of approximately three thousand people.

Since the 1970s many Sassani have found employment in the factories that have cropped up in the town's industrial zone. This area has seen strong growth in the last twenty years because of tax incentives, cheap labor, and the government connections of local officials. Also present in the village is a small group of artisans and self-employed entrepreneurs. About 50 percent of the full-time wage earners own small plots of land in the surrounding countryside, and farming is a weekend or holiday activity that contributes to the family larder.

This chapter begins the ethnography of Sasso by situating the town within its larger social and cultural history. Before doing so, however, it will be useful to have some understanding of the fieldwork upon which this study is based. My primary trip to Sasso took place between February of 1993 and March of 1994; it involved extensive participant/observation research and both formal and informal interviews. I returned to Sasso in the summer of 1996 to videotape the promenade,[2] and I spent many hours with Sassani watching the tapes and using them as a springboard for discussing the promenade. On both trips I stayed with relatives, my aunt Linda (a widow in her late sixties), and my aunt Norina and uncle Michele and their three adult children. More than generous hosts, these families helped me to gain inroads into the social life of Sasso. While I performed research on the promenade almost every night, some of my most suggestive participant/observation data emerged in mundane activities such as drinking coffee at cafés, conversing with shopkeepers, sharing family meals, and taking car rides. My aunts were particularly important for my research, and though this study is intended as a general portrait of contemporary Sasso, I found myself focusing greater attention on women's culture. In special events like picnics, visits with family or friends, or trips to the cemetery – as well as in ordinary practices like gardening, grocery shopping, food preparation, and soap-opera viewing – I gained a deeper appreciation for the experiences of Sassano women. This emphasis is especially apparent in chapter 4, which discusses gender roles in Sassano culture, and chapter 5, which looks carefully at the technical details of the passeggiata, an event usually associated with women.

All the translations of interviews and Italian publications in this work are my own. In everyday talk, Sassani constantly shift back and forth between standard Italian and the province's Abruzzese dialect. While I am fluent in standard Italian, Abruzzese is my mother tongue, and I employed both forms of speech during my research. In this study I have made no effort to alter regional expressions and have remained true to Sassano usage in all direct quotations.

PORTRAIT OF AN ITALIAN PROVINCE

Sasso is located in the Abruzzo, a province situated on the Adriatic coast across the Italian peninsula from Rome. From a geographical standpoint, the Abruzzo straddles the line between the North and South and thus occupies a liminal space in the regional debates of Italian politics. While some maintain that the province belongs to *il Mezzogiorno* (literally, "the midday," the region that runs from Sicily to the area just south of Rome), others situate it in *il Centro-Nord* (the Center-North region), distancing it from the South and its reputation for underdevelopment (Mutti 1994).

The Abruzzo and the Southern provinces, however, share a common historical and cultural past. From 1140 to 1860 most of the provinces stretching from Naples to Sicily were dominated variously by the Normans, Aragons, and Bourbons and experienced centuries of oppression and political domination (Barzini 1964). It was only a few decades after Italian unification in 1861 that the Abruzzo emerged as an autonomous entity. Before then, the province was called the Abruzzi (plural) and included what is now the Molise area, a province that is unambiguously seen as part of *il Mezzogiorno*.

Many students of *la questione del Sud* (The Southern Question) believe that the region's current difficulties are rooted in centuries of foreign domination and tyrannical feudal regimes that ruled the area until the mid-nineteenth century (Bohlen 1996). To this day, such commentators argue, the culture of the South is marked by a "briganti" (outlaw) mentality – a lack of faith in civic institutions, the use of quasi-legal survival strategies in everyday behavior, a large black-market economy, and pervasive crime (Barzini 1964; Bohlen 1996). After the Second World War, the Italian government established a state agency called *la Cassa del Mezzogiorno* (The Midday Region Fund) to spur Southern economic development. Its programs, however, fell far short of their goals. Millions of dollars were sent southward for ambitious public works projects, and much of it was wasted in corruption and mismanagement. As journalist Celestine Bohlen observed, the landscape of the South is "filled with unfinished highways with clover leafs that go nowhere, hospitals that never opened, and factories that never started hiring" (Bohlen 1996, A8). While the national government's development programs have been notorious for their corruption, representations such as Bohlen's distort the complex relationships between the regions of Italy. The journalist Sergio Turone, for example, has pointed out that it is the Northern provinces, not the Southern ones, that have the highest incidents of political corruption (Turone 1993).[3]

In the Abruzzo, the ruling Democratic Christian leaders have chosen to distance themselves from both an identification with the South and the overall politics of regionalism. They have done this by promoting a discourse of modernization and ecotourism. In 1986 the Abruzzo's regional council passed a law to support the protection of environmental resources and was given a special mandate to develop a system of natural parks and high-tech enterprises. In keeping with national directives, the government decided to devote a third of the Abruzzo's land to the national wildlife parks in the Maiella and Gran Sasso areas while supporting new companies involved in nuclear technology and communication services. These efforts sought to spur the economy and provide a more modern image to the province, which had traditionally been associated with agriculture and subsistence farming. By the 1990s the Abruzzo had industrialized more rapidly than any of the Southern provinces (Mutti 1994).

Development, however, has not just been important for the Abruzzo but for the country as a whole, and this issue is intimately tied with that of outmigration. In the first part of the twentieth century, Italy was far from a modern nation. While there were advancements made in the "production of cars, steel, electrical energy, and artificial fibers," (Ginsborg 1990, 210) these developments were confined mainly to the Northwest, and "most Italians still earned a living, if they earned it all, in traditional sectors of the economy: in small, labour intensive firms ... small shops, and trades [and] in agriculture" (Ginsborg 1990, 210). Electricity and indoor plumbing only became widely available in rural areas in late 1960s. The Second World War compounded the problems of underdevelopment. The chronic unemployment and lack of prospects for a better future during this period lead more than a million Italians to seek work in Argentina, Canada, the United States, Australia, and Venezuela (Ginsborg 1990, 211), where there was a great demand for manual labor. Unlike the exodus of the 1880s, which was largely composed of poor landless peasants, most of the people who emigrated after the Second World War were artisans, small landowners, and people with a certain level of technical expertise (Bolino 1973; Ginsborg 1990), and "nearly 70% of those who left were from the South" Ginsborg explains (211).[4] A great many Italians also sought their fortunes in Northern Europe, especially France, Switzerland, and Belgium. While some gravitated toward France because of its dire need of rebuilding, others went looking for employment in Switzerland, which had amassed economic wealth through its neutrality. Belgium offered steady but often hazardous work in the coal mining industry. Though a portion of those who left were men hired to do short-term contract work, those who had secured long-term work often sent for wives, children, and relatives and eventually took up residence in their new host countries. My father, Giovanni Fiore Del Negro, was one of those men who left his village in 1948 to go work in the coal mines of Belgium. After returning to Italy for a brief stint, my father left for Ontario, Canada, where he first worked in a metal refinery. A few months later he was hired as a laborer on the construction site of the Toronto airport. He finally decided to settle in Quebec because of his familiarity with the French language.

The years between 1950 and 1970 are often referred to as the period of Italy's "economic miracle." As Ginsborg notes, however, this era's prosperity did little to improve living conditions for the citizens in Central or Southern Italy (Ginsborg 1990, 212). While manufacturing increased sixfold and the urban centers in the industrial triangle between Genoa, Milan, and Turin produced consumer goods like Olivetti typewriters, Fiat cars, and Candy washing machines (Ginsborg 1990), the Abruzzo saw a sharp decline in agriculture and the massive depopulation of its rural areas (Bolino 1973). The significance of this demographic crises cannot be overestimated. The Abruzzo had one of the highest rates of emigration, and, in Sasso alone, fully half of the residents left, many resettling in Canada or the United States. In one of the few studies that examines the sociological aspects of the Abruzzese diaspora in the mid-twentieth century, Giuseppe Bolino (1973) reveals that, accounting for both departures and returns, approximately forty thousand people left the Abruzzo in the four years immediately following the Second World War (Bolino 1973, 47). According to historian Filippo Mazzonis, "from unification to the First World War 700,000 Abruzzese had emigrated permanently, and after the Second World War, an estimated total of 450,000 more left [for almost] the combined total of the inhabitants of the region" (Mazzonis 1994, 183).

What specific set of material and social conditions prompted the Abruzzese to seek a life in other lands? Constantino Felice's book *Il disagio di vivere: Il cibo, la casa, le malattie in Abruzzo e Molise dall'unità al secondo dopoguerra* (1989) is remarkably enlightening in this regard. In this Annal School-inspired study of the food, shelter, hygiene, and everyday existence of the peoples of Abruzzo and Molise, Felice clearly describes how in the Second World War the heavily bombarded Abruzzesi cities of Pescara, Sulmona, Avezzano, and Teramo suffered huge losses in human life and economic infrastructure. The systematic attacks upon these areas not only made fertile land unusable but contributed to the destruction of livestock, olive orchards, and hydraulic plants, which were crucial for the survival of the region's inhabitants. The death toll and destruction of property was enormous.[5] The disorganization in the means of transportation, drop in fish production, lack of proper housing, and inefficient distribution of goods all made the early years after the Second World War fraught with difficulty (Felice 1989). Inflation, rises in the cost of staples, and unemployment (Felice 1989), coupled with the growing confrontations between the Communist and Democratic Christian Parties (which sometimes led to casualties and even deaths), only served to exacerbate the pre-existing climate of political and social instability. Repressive work conditions in the countryside made the desperate search for *pane e lavoro* (bread and work) a dangerous proposition. For example, in March of 1950 in the small Abruzzese town of Lentella, the police shot two peasants in the field because of a confrontation with their padrone (boss) (Felice 1989, 313). Those who flocked to the urban centers of the North in hopes of improving their lot were often equally exploited: they lived in shanty houses and worked ten- to twelve-hour days without any proper labor rights or legal representation.

It is clear that the end of the Second World War had raised Italians' expectations for a better life, but in the late 1940s and the early 1950s, the economic picture in the Abruzzo and the other Central and Southern provinces looked bleak. Many of the casualties from the war – fighters from the resistance, mine victims, soldiers returning from war camps or prisons – came back to desolate, war-ravaged villages (Bolino 1973). According to Felice, the postwar reconstruction of the late 1940s and 1950s, often called *la rinascita* (the rebirth), failed to substantially raise the standard of living or absorb the surplus labor force. In the beginning of the rinascita, Felice explains, many Italians were proactive and hopeful. They joined political parties and participated in union struggles. They aspired to owning *"il pezzo di terra,"* (a small patch of land) and having *"il posto"* (a secure job) (Felice 1989, 314), but their ambitions were quickly dashed in the years immediately after the war and they looked toward other countries for a better future. When the Italian economy finally began to improve, regional differences were substantial. In his "pioneering study [*Le tre Italie* (1977)], sociologist Arnaldo Bagnasco identifie[s] not one but three Italies: the Northwest, characterized by conurbations, large-scale factories and a well developed service sector; the Northeast and Center, characterized by small-scale industrialization and persistence of primary and social networks"; and the South, which he refers to as *la terza Italia* (the third Italy), to appearances "modernized" but in its economy underdeveloped (Bull 2001, 57). While the economy of the Northwest picked up in the early 1950s, it was not until the 1960s that what has often been called Italy's "economic miracle" began to bear its fruit in the Northeast/Central region or the South. This period of greater prosperity paved the way for the "growth of consumerism and the development of the media, particularly that of television" (Bull 2001, 55).

The Abruzzo province benefited from the economic upsurge that Italy experienced in the 1960s, and in many ways postwar Sasso is a case study in the modernization of rural Italy. In this period, corporate investment and economic development turned what had been an agricultural community into a local center of light industry. The former Sassano contadini (peasants) were transformed into the impiegati[6] (wage earners) of the modern labor force, and the town's former mayor, Guido Lantenari, was key in mustering support for his town. A well-known Democratic Christian, he held a number of posts in the national government, and his political connections have been partially responsible for Sasso's growth. Cheap labor and subsidies from *la Cassa del Mezzogiorno* also helped pave the way for the development of the town's industrial base; they supply greater opportunities for steady employment for the residents of Sasso and the surrounding towns. In a culture of contentious village rivalries, Sassani had long thought of their town as more urban and advanced than its neighbors; with its newfound economic prowess, their cosmopolitan attitudes were given a modern industrial base upon which to thrive. As we shall see in chapter 3, the town's economic privilege has exacerbated local conflicts and increased resentments from the nearby communities.

Throughout Italy, the economic successes of the 1960s led to a phenomenon that historians call "remigration," the return of immigrants to their home country. Though the dominant narrative of immigration in the American mass media is of the oppressed and impoverished masses leaving Europe for freedom and prosperity in the United States, many Italian immigrants did not understand their experiences in that way. To the contrary, those who left Italy in the decades after the Second World War often did so with the intent of returning, either when they had made their fortunes in foreign lands or when Italy's own economy had improved. Such intentions were not passing fancies. During the period of separation, many immigrants kept in touch with their extended families in Sasso through letters, occasional telephone calls and trips, and, most importantly, a steady stream of cheques. Some of those who moved to wealthier countries like Canada or the United States and were lucky enough to have buildup sufficient savings bought homes in Sasso and returned there to re-establish their lives, vacation, or retire. Those who did not fare so well abroad were lured back by Italy's economic progress. In my extended family for example, my first cousin Carmela and her husband, my uncle Federico, his wife, and teenage son, and my aunt Linda and her husband all invested in property and returned to Italy to enjoy their retirements. What is perhaps most interesting about this phenomenon is that, in all of these cases, the reimmigrants left children and grandchildren behind to come back to their native land.

This history of economic difficulties, eventual modernization, immigration, and remigration plays a key role in Sassani's vision of their town. During its major waves of migration in the last 150 years (the 1880s to the 1920s, and 1946 to the 1960s) outmigration from Italy was the most tangible symptom of the economic and political malaise that had affected the country. This was perhaps most profoundly illustrated in the painting of Giorgio de Chirico, whose stark images of empty public spaces captured the sense of loneliness and despair engendered by Italy's underdevelopment and shrinking populations. However, the return of the immigrants in the beginning of the 1970s held complex meaning for Sassani. In one sense, it illustrated the prosperity that Sasso and post-1960s Italy in general had achieved. But because many migrants kept close ties with the homeland, their return was less indicative of a totally new set of social circumstances than it was the culmination of a longstanding project, a detour in the immigrant's lives that had finally been completed. Remigration, after all, was not a new phenomenon in Italy, and, like many other Abruzzesi, my grandparent's generation clearly remember townsfolk returning from migration overseas.[7] While all Sassani were happy to see their piazza lose its lonely, de Chirico-like emptiness, and, while some returning immigrants were happy to have been taken back into the bosom of their town, others had more ambivalent feelings. For example, Paolo Del Cerchio, a man I interviewed during my fieldwork, immigrated from Sasso to a small city in Switzerland in his late twenties and did not come back until his fifties. While he never felt fully at home in Switzerland, his experiences abroad distanced him from Italy, and he told me that since he has returned, he has felt betwixt and between, neither fully Swiss nor fully Italian. The patterns of outmigration also affected the experiences of those who stayed behind. As I shall explain in detail below, the notions of modernity and cosmopolitanism were central to the townsfolk's self-image in the period of my fieldwork. Sassani represent their town as a modern one, a place that has combined the best of small-town living with the best of the modern urban experience. In the context of migration, Sassani's emphasis on cosmopolitanism can be partially seen as a reaction to the worldly, traveled experiences of the returning migrants, a defensive response to the presence of their better-traveled paesani ("distant family relative" or "member of one's village"). Further, the immigrant's return was read as a kind of validation of Sasso's success. Pointing to the rimpatriati (repatriates),[8] Sassani could proudly say that their townsfolk had been all over the world and succeeded in foreign countries but had always maintained their family ties and, in the end, had chosen to live in their hometown.

This history of migration and remigration has not only informed Sassani's images of their own town, it has also shaped their ideas about Italy's urban centers and the New World. For example, Sassani's vision of "La Merica"[9] is ambivalent. While many see North America as the land of opportunity and freedom, they are also all too aware of i sacrifici (the sacrifices) immigration entails – cultural isolation, strenuous work, low wages, and long periods of absence from family and friends. The central Italian cities of Chieti, Pescara, and Teramo elicit a similar ambivalence. These urban centers are viewed as places where people go to work and improve their chances of upward mobility. Despite the attractions of the nearby cities, Sassano ties to the village remain strong. Those who relocated for employment have longstanding filial attachments; many still own land in the town and make periodic visits to friends and family, especially during the summer and the patron-Saint feast days. Further, many Sassani feel at least a measure of disdain toward "La Merica." They resent its economic power and what they see as its vapid consumerism and crass materialism. This is not to say that those who criticize "La Merica" romanticize Italy. Against the more utopic visions of il paese (the village) and a desire to be reunited with parents or retire in their native land, there are those like my father who have little faith in the Italian government and its ability to provide its citizen's with a descent way of life. The poverty my father suffered as a young boy in 1920s and 1930s is still alive in his memory, and he has never considered moving back to Italy permanently. While the rimpatriati (repatriates) who have moved back to live in Sasso and the nearby centers are occasionally seen as arrogant, many of the returnees are retired pensioners who lead quiet and unassuming lives. Indeed, many Sassani look upon these returnees with respect and understand the hard choices they have had to make along the way. For example, young Sassano married men with children who have had to go away periodically to work in Northern Italy or different parts of Europe to support their families are all too familiar with the larger social conditions of unemployment and economic scarcity that lead early generations to seek their fortunes elsewhere.[10]

While the economic gains of the post-1960s era encouraged the outmigrants to return, the province's economic success was overshadowed in the early 1990s by political problems. In 1992, the executive council of the Abruzzo was investigated for corruption, and dozens of provincial officials were accused of mismanaging European development funds. Turone (1993) has suggested that this provincial scandal led directly to the tangentopoli (literally, bribesville) affair, a political crisis that revealed systemic corruption in the highest levels of the Italian national government. During this tumultuous period, many dissatisfied Abruzzesi, who had historically voted for the Democratic Christians, gave their support to the far-right New Alliance Party (formerly the neofascist Movimento Sociale Italiano), and one town even elected a neofascist mayor.

In the early days of the *mani pulite* (literally, clean hands operation; the official investigation of the tangentopoli affair), all of the members of the Abruzzo's executive council were jailed, and many were forced to resign. The town of Sasso also received its share of media attention. Both Italian and French television networks did extensive investigative pieces on mayor Lantenari, his connections in the national government, and the town's political corruption. Sasso was held up as an object lesson in tangentopoli and an example of the festering moral decay of a failing bureaucratic system. Accusations of raccomandazione (clientalism) and unfair hiring practices in Sasso made national headlines. The local scandal reached its peak in the summer of 1993 when twenty-seven officials from the municipal government were served with subpoenas and held under house arrest.

Like the changing economic and demographic situations, the emergence of the tangentopoli situation was deeply felt by Sassani. It cast a pall over the economic achievements that the previous decades had seen and engendered both a sense of shame and insecurity. Had Sasso's prosperity, many wondered, been nothing but the product of corruption and deceit? Was a return of bad economic times around the corner? The worst images of Italy – as land of poverty, stagnation, and corruption – were evoked by this turn of events, and, as we shall see in later chapters, they played a key role in Sasso's self-image.

The changes that have occurred in the economic and political landscape in the last thirty years have been accompanied by changing ideas about gender. In traditional Italian society, women were often judged on their ability to maintain a tidy and efficient household; domestic talents were highly valued by the community and considered an important asset for a potential wife. Men, on the other hand, were praised for their industriousness and valued according to their potential as a breadwinner. Perhaps most striking were traditional beliefs about sexuality. Women were thought of as having enormous sexual powers that they alone were responsible for regulating. So strong was this force that for a woman to even appear in public was seen as a potentially provocative act. As a result, space was highly gendered, with the public domain given over to men while women were to remain in the domestic sphere. Young women were discouraged from going out unchaperoned, and even older or married women knew that they must remain unobtrusive in public, lest they be seen as promiscuous and bring shame to their families (Del Negro 1997).

Traditional gender roles still persist, but much has changed in Sasso. Young women now date at an earlier age and go out dancing unaccompanied by relatives, and, while some older widows still wear *il lutto* (black mourning garb) until the day they die, others return to everyday clothing. Furthermore, the public sphere is no longer a male domain. More and more women seek out careers in business or go far from home to study, and a small group of highly respected, female professionals has emerged in Sasso. Despite these changes, men and women still do not enjoy the same rights and privileges. Even the emergence of female professionals has not altered the common expectation that women will fulfill themselves through marriage and family, and the wedding day is still understood as a pivotal moment in a woman's life. Men's promiscuity and sexual dalliances are tolerated and even encouraged, while women are severely stigmatized for openly engaging in premarital relations. Although men are encouraged to marry and settle down, there is a greater responsibility to *sistemare la figlia femmina* (settle the female child) and make her a respectable member of society. In so doing, the parents have fulfilled their obligations and removed any threat of shame that may tarnish their daughter's reputation or their own place in the community.

"OUR LITTLE PARIS"

In the local imagination, Sasso has often been viewed as a modern, cosmopolitan village with close affinities to the nearby coastal centers. The townsfolk affectionately call it *la piccola Parigi dell' Abruzzo* (the little Paris of the Abruzzo) and point to its attractive thoroughfare and well-known passeggiata as a sign of the town's *civiltà* (civility, politeness, public spirit).[11] As a forum for discussing social change, the passeggiata can be understood as an example of what Milton Singer has called a "cultural performance" (1972). In his usage, cultural performance is a broad category that can include readings of religious texts, lectures, festivals, plays, social gatherings, and a wide range of public rituals and other display events. What these happenings have in common, Singer suggests, is that in India they have provided an arena for discussing the meanings of modernity. As the centerpiece of the local culture and an icon of Sasso's urban sophistication, the passeggiata serves the same function in Sasso that folk dramas and religious festivals do in Singer's India.[12]

Figure 1 Sidewalk bar along *il corso* (video still from the author's field tapes)

Figure 2 Another bar (video still from the author's field tapes)

Figure 3   Women taking their vasche (laps) (video still from the author's field tapes)

Sassani usually begin the passeggiata by walking down to the piazza and chatting with friends. While men typically relax in sidewalk cafés and bars, women perform their ritual vasche (laps) up and down the town's main street (figures 1–3). In this lively, cinematic atmosphere, "greetings, glances, gestures, costume, and conversations" intertwine to create a richly textured canvas of meaning (Silverman 1975, 67; see also Pitkin 1993). Although everyone takes part in the passeggiata, its most ardent participants are young women. Boisterously parading up and down the main thoroughfare, the passeggiata provides women of marriageable age with a socially sanctioned opportunity for flirting and courting. Parents encourage children to participate in the event, and the rhetorical skills learned in the piazza become useful in the marriage market, the work place, and the complex politics of the town. Though the term passeggiata literally means "promenade" and specifically refers to the period of piazza strolling between five thirty and eight p.m., Sassani often use this word as a broad concept to refer to any kind of leisure or play. During the week, the passeggiata announces the end of the workday and allows Sassani to share a moment of sociability before the family dinner. The Sunday promenade (figures 4–5) is a more condensed version of the event, lasting anywhere from one to two hours, depending on the mood and disposition of the participants.

Figure 4   Leaving the church for the Sunday passeggiata (promenade) (video still from the author's field tapes)

Figure 5   Children playing on the Sunday passeggiata (video still from the author's field tapes)

Figure 6   Older women viewing the passeggiata from their terrace (video still from the author's field tapes)

While the weekday passeggiata takes place in the evening before supper, the Sunday passeggiata follows church and tends to be more family oriented. Parents and children walk hand-in-hand and Sassani who are seldom seen about the town during the week accompany their families to the piazza and pleasantly socialize with other towns-folk. During mass, men tend to stand in the back of the church. Some slip outside to smoke and talk with friends, while others can be found in the coffee bars playing cards and drinking. On this religious "day of rest," housewives are often at home preparing fresh pasta and laboring over the Sunday meal. Typically, older married women attend services at five in the evening, when they get to spend a few hours of uninterrupted time with their female friends.

The passeggiata reaches its peak during the summer months. At this time, immigrants, returning students, and a small group of out-siders who come to the Abruzzo for vacations swell the ranks in the piazza and give the event a particularly festive mood. The temperate weather also draws Sasso's older citizens into the piazza. Sitting on tiny wicker chairs normally used near the fireplace, these inveterate spectators observe the passeggiata from stoops, terraces, or balconies (figure 6). During this season, the after-supper passeggiata may run late into the evening and involves more loitering and conversation then walking. As the evening wears down, the event becomes more

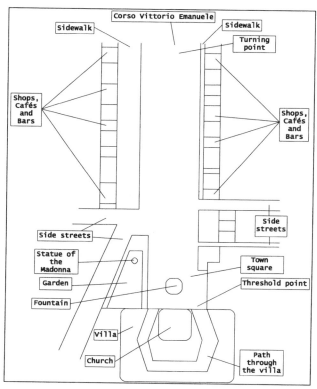

Figure 7   Diagram of the piazza in Sasso

male-dominated; women return home, and the piazza becomes a center of male cavorting, drinking, and card-playing. The late night is also a time for intimate rendezvous. Meeting in the public park behind the church, couples share a moment of quiet and romance in a place that is both public and secluded.

THE CULTURAL GEOGRAPHY OF SASSO'S PIAZZA

Just as the times of the day and the seasons of the year are given cultural meanings, so are the physical spaces of the piazza. Sasso's main thoroughfare, Corso Vittorio Emanuele, terminates in a town square and a fountain, behind which lie the church of San Michele and the villa, a carefully landscaped arboretum (figures 7–8). A medieval town with large fortress walls (figure 9), today's Sasso is the product of hundreds of years of construction and reconstruction. Originally the center of town was located in what is now called

Figure 8   Corso Vittorio Emanuele (video still from the author's field tapes)

Figure 9   Postcard of Sasso illustrating its old fortress walls (Ed. Gasparia-Riv.Tab. n. 1)

Figure 10   Postcard of the Church of San Michele (Ed. Gasparia-Riv.Tab. n. 1)

Sasso's "old quarter." The landslides of the 1880s, however, destroyed many homes, and subsequent development shifted the town's center in the direction of the current piazza. The villa was built in the early 1900s, and its shrubbery and geometrical design appear to be inspired by the English natural style of the period. In the 1960s the old San Michele church was torn down and rebuilt, and an octagonal fountain was added to the square (figure 10).[13]

Unlike the narrow streets found elsewhere in Sasso, the main corso is broad and open, recalling the landscaping of the grand boulevards of Europe's nineteenth-century cities. In the design of its downtown and its public endorsement of "people watching," Sasso embodies a distinctly modern and urban sensibility. Walter Benjamin's nineteenth-century flâneur (a city stroller who walks the streets to study the crowd) would feel quite at home in this milieu (Benjamin 1989).[14] In this public sphere modern, urban spectacting and capitalist consumption come together to produce a moving tableaux of contemporary Italian social life.

Near the fountain, a bank, a gas pump, and the balconies of private homes overlook one side of *il corso*; across the street a Madonna sits in a small v-shaped park. Moving further from the church, various boutiques, cafés, bars, newspaper stands, and fruit shops line the broad boulevard. At the far end are found the police station and city hall. While the term "piazza" literally means "town square," it is usually used in Sasso to refer to the entire area from the villa to the police station.

The tree-lined corso is slightly concave, and, as a result, the force of gravity subtly pulls the strollers back toward the center when they reach the end of the piazza. From such a vantage point, the entire downtown can be visually experienced as a cinematic whole. As Sassani stop here to turn and resume their walking in the other direction, they are rewarded with a momentary snapshot of the square – a painterly image that emphasizes distance and perspective and contributes to the aesthetics of strolling. During this pause, time stands still, resuming only when the walker breaks the frame to undertake yet another lap across the thoroughfare. This quick interruption in the forward momentum of strolling builds a small wedge of stillness into the flow of the event, and the movement of the crowd is experienced against the sensation of one's own motionlessness. While the passeggiata involves periodic stoppings and goings, it is at the margins of the piazza that the notions of separateness and togetherness, individuality and membership in a community, become most apparent. At this juncture, participants often decide whether to continue strolling or return home.

In everyday life, Sassani use bodily metaphors to bring meaning to the social space of the piazza. The church and the villa are often referred to as *il capo*, (dialect for "the head"), while the lower half of the piazza and the area beyond it are called *quart da peda*, (dialect for "side by the feet"). The capo is usually reserved for quiet conversation with friends and reflective meditation. In the villa (figures 11–12), strollers pause to admire the panoramic vista of the nearby villages and the lush hilltop vegetation so characteristic of the Abruzzese landscape. In this "head" region, Sassani customarily seek out moments of peaceful introspection and respite from the hustle and bustle of modern life. This is where people come to think and focus upon things of the mind, away from the distractions of the world; it is the mental and spiritual center of the body politic.

Leaving the quiet, intimate villa, Sassani enter a bustling social scene and focus their attention on the behavior of those around them. Thick with visual stimuli, the activities of *il corso* revolve around social interaction and the key practices of seeing and being seen. If the head of the piazza is a place for reason and piety, the "side by the feet" is meant for the sensual pleasures of life. In the area above, religion and nature reign supreme, while the area below is clearly devoted to the secular activities of commerce and cheap amusements. Here, the terms "head" and "feet" are more than fanciful local descriptions; they are ways of endowing different parts of the piazza with specific

Figure 11   Path through the villa (video still from the author's field tapes)

Figure 12   An intimate moment in the villa (video still from the author's field tapes)

meanings and values. As a metaphor, "capo" and *"quart da peda"* provide Sassani with a blueprint for social action, a blueprint that the townsfolk implicitly invoke every time they utter the words or stroll on *il corso*.

Bodily metaphors not only help Sassani to navigate the piazza in socially acceptable ways, they also define the physical boundaries of the passeggiata. In Sasso, everybody knows that one's strolling should end at a specific spot in the *quart da peda* just south of the city

Figure 13   A family leaves the "turning point" while a couple approaches it
(video still from the author's field tapes)

hall. (This spot is labeled as the "turning point," see figures 7 and 13).
To go beyond the turning point is to exit the public performance of
the passeggiata. When people reach this spot, they turn around in a
seamless, choreographed manner and resume their vasche down the
thoroughfare in the opposite direction. Locals humorously call this
maneuver "the changing of the guard." I first discovered the turning
point by accident. Strolling the piazza on one of my first evenings in
town, I was accompanied by my friends Pietro and Maria. Lost in
conversation, I walked past the turning point and found myself alone;
my two companions had turned around and were laughing at the
spectacle of a lone walker, talking to herself in the non-passeggiata
zone of the *quart da peda*.

PRE-PASSEGGIATA PREPARATION

While Sassani use images of the body to describe the piazza, they
often use dramaturgical metaphors in portraying the passeggiata
itself. Here, Corso Vittorio Emanuele is a stage, the promenade is
Sasso's greatest public spectacle, and the townsfolk make up the
ensemble cast. Like all actors, Sassani take great care in grooming
and costuming themselves for their performances. And it is here, in
the "backstage area" of the home (Goffman 1959) that the passeggiata
begins for most Sassani.

The women with whom I did research always took great pains to make sure they were presentabili (presentable, suitably dressed) and *in ordine* (neat, tidy, well put together) for the passeggiata. For Emilia, a twenty-two-year-old student, a typical pre-passeggiata routine involved showering or a quick bidet cleaning, applying eyeliner and blush, and changing from a casual tuta (jogging suit) into more formal attire. This costume usually consisted of straight-leg jeans, a body suit, shirt or sweater, and a sports jacket. For her passeggiata outings, Marina, a young school teacher, usually wore comfortable stirrup pants or casual slacks, which she embellished with snug sweaters and tailored jackets. With her costume in place, mascara, eyeliner, and blush would be applied with great care. While their choice of makeup varied, the women I observed invariably completed their cosmetic preparations with an application of lipstick. In so doing, they dramatically marked their anticipated transition from the private sphere of the home to the public domain of the piazza.

While the act of applying lipstick delineates the end of the pre-passeggiata preparation, the stroller's special attire frames the promenade itself. A clear example of Bauman's keying of performance (1977), the donning of finer clothes helps strollers experience the passeggiata as a special time and indicates to the rest of the town that they take the event seriously. In general, the women I observed marked the event by mixing and matching formal and casual pieces. Exploring differing combinations of clothes and accessories, they varied their appearance from night to night and demonstrated their sartorial creativity. The passeggiata performers know that they are going to be scrutinized by other townsfolk and they, in turn, go to the piazza to see and be seen. All participants are expected to make a token effort to look presentabili, and all of the women I knew changed some aspects of their appearance before they went out – even if it meant only applying lipstick.

The amount of time participants devote to the primping and preening before the passeggiata, however, is a function of work, marital status, gender, age, and personality. One middle-aged, married secretary, upon returning from her job at the liceo (college) at the end of the day would routinely change into a new sweater or a flattering jacket before heading for the piazza. She did this as a matter of course and barely looked herself over in the mirror. On the other hand Dina, a single woman in her early twenties, would spend considerably more time ascertaining her appearance. Unlike Teresa, the secretary, she clearly had more time to devote to refining her overall look.

In Sasso young, single women are encouraged to put their charms on display. Married women are also held to the standards of female beauty but expected to look more like *una donna seria* (a serious woman). While men also experiment with their apparel and enjoy the pleasures of adornment, there is less social pressure on them to look good. As we will see in chapter 5, it is women who are the focus of attention and are judged for their performance of *bella figura* (cutting a fine figure) and disinvoltura (poise, ease of manners).

My aunt Norina, a married woman in her mid-fifties, seldom took the weekday promenade and reserved her elaborate bathing and dressing ritual for her Sunday church outings. As with many of the older women who attended services, the "tailleur" (French for "tailor-made suit") was the clothing of choice. Both practical and elegant, the tailleur could be made to look more or less formal. With an expensive blouse, jewelry, high heels, and a scarf, the tailleur can create an extremely dressy effect; wearing the jacket alone with a simple skirt and sweater, the stroller can produce a more casual look. My aunt proudly told me that she had gotten a great deal of use from her professionally sewn, gaberdine suit. On late Sunday afternoons, she would typically tease and spray her hair, apply her *Ballo di Notte* (Evening Ball) cologne and a pale shade of lipstick. She mindfully completed her transformation by reaching into her jewelry box and putting on her finest gold chain necklace and bracelet.

At home, these private cosmetic alterations were also accompanied by subtle, yet palpable changes in attitude. In the backstage regions of the village, Sassani symbolically shed aspects of the work self and enter the ludic frame of mind. In my aunt Norina's house, the mood of relaxation would prevail as my cousins and I prepared for our evening diversion. There was a visible break in our daily schedules; running water, sounds of blow dryers, fragrant perfumes, and light-hearted banter echoed the growing hustle and bustle from the piazza. Students, last minute shoppers, and buses full of workers make the downtown progressively busier, and the mundane piazza becomes a place where one can briefly escape from the worries of the day. In inclement weather, the die-hard passeggiata goers were depressed by their empty piazza and viscerally affected by the absence of movement in the downtown area (figure 14). When I heard people describe the sense of desolation at the sight of an empty piazza, I couldn't help but think of de Chirico's 1914 painting, "Mystery and Melancholy of a Street."

The sartorial richness of the promenade gives the event a distinctively theatrical quality. Knowing what to wear and how to wear it in this context is not a simple matter. The notions of *vestito per dentro* (inside wear) and *vestito per fuori* (outside wear) help Sassani split up the fashion universe into two basic categories. When "inside wear" is called for, one's style is characterized by a neglectful appearance and an almost conspicuous lack of attention to the details of dress;

Figure 14   The empty piazza (video still from the author's field tapes)

when "outside wear" is in order, there is a greater concern for clothing and comportment. Before leaving the house for even the most mundane errand, Sassani will change into outside wear; upon returning home, they will change back into inside wear or cover their finer clothes with tute (jogging suits) or other layers of protective clothing. While North Americans may make a distinction between children's school clothes and their play clothes or adults' work clothes and their casual attire, the Sassano distinction between *vestito per dentro* and *vestito per fuori* (and the common practice of changing clothes several times a day) is far more rigid and reveals a culturally specific set of ideas about the importance of clothing and appearance in everyday life. The sharp dichotomy is at least partially a survival of Sasso's agricultural past. The tuta of today's young women is the contemporary equivalent of the grembiule, a knee-length smock worn in Sasso's pre-industrial past by women to protect their clothes from the ravages of time and labor intensive domestic work. The long tradition of hand sewing in rural Italy and the widespread popularity of the designer fashion industry has also helped foster Sassani's deep appreciation for expensive, custom-tailored clothing.

In their habits of consumption, Sassani generally prefer to spend more money on a few fine pieces of clothes than to have a large wardrobe of mediocre items. Only occasionally do Sassani spend their money at the market or the nearby discount store for bargain attire. The people with whom I worked tended to spend money on moderately priced fashions from designers like Max Mara or Fila. Voicing a typical attitude, Antonietta told me that she would rather spend 250,000 Lire (about $200 US) for an attractive and long-lasting Moschino sweater than have three or four ugly tops from *il mercato* (the local market). Like precious resources, these items were exploited to their fullest potential; Sassani removed them immediately upon returning home and cared for them with enormous diligence. Even if a finer item is worn frequently, most Sassani will cover it in plastic before they place it in the closet, and newer clothes are frequently covered in older clothes before they are hung up. Shopping expeditions occurred perhaps once or twice a year around special holidays and celebrations, when gift money was most available for sartorial expenditures. Those with more limited incomes either purchased less expensive items from the stores in the area or had moderately priced suits made by the local tailors.

Despite their concern with proper attire, Sassani paid little attention to how they looked in the domestic sphere. Here, the townsfolk frequently preferred to wear ill-fitting or damaged clothes and were considerably less aware of their bodies and their overall demeanor than they were in the piazza. But how do Sassani differ from North Americans who lounge around their homes in sweat pants? The difference is that Sassani are far less likely to go out with their *vestito per dentro* and almost always change clothes before going on the most mundane errand. To appear in "inside wear" in public is a sign of disrespect to others. Frequently shifting from public to private on weekends, it would not be uncommon for a Sassano to change outfits three or four times in one day. Lina, a woman who attends university in Rome, told me that, in the city, she would often run errands wearing her most shabby clothes; however in Sasso, she said, she would never dare commit such a crime. Without the anonymity that the big city provides, any foray into the public sphere may lead to an encounter with relatives or co-workers. As a result, there is greater pressure to comply with the rules of dress and public decorum in Sasso. Here, the dynamics of small-town life combine with the culture's strong valuation of appearance to sharpen the distinction between "inner wear" and "outer wear."

If the public sphere requires of Sassani a heightened attention to appearance, then the promenade brings this emphasis to its zenith. Here, one is always an object of intense scrutiny and judgment. For the passeggiata to operate as an expressive event, each member of the town must take responsibility for their respective part in the collective performance. To go on the promenade is to enter into a contractual agreement with others and to tacitly consent to contribute to the town's *bella figura*. The strongest criticism that one can deliver of another's appearance is "*Che sciamurato!*" – an Abruzzesi expression that means both "How disheveled!" and "How rude!" Being sciamurato on the passeggiata not only tarnishes one's own reputation,

Figure 15   Zia Norina (author's photograph)

it literally makes the town look bad and is taken as an affront to the community. As we will see in chapter 5, social actors must demonstrate a certain level of sartorial competence to adequately participate in the promenade.

The rules of dress and decorum are most strongly enforced by the older women in the community, and their scrutiny begins in the preparatory stages of the event. During my last six months in Sasso, I stayed with a family of butchers whose apartments were located in the same building as their shop. My Aunt Norina, the matriarch of the clan, would insist that my cousins and I appear before her in the butcher store before going out on the promenade (figure 15). This brief display provided my aunt and her employees with a moment of respite from the tedium of work. Norina's comments were frequently critical, exhorting me to adjust my jacket or telling my cousin that her sweater clashed with her pants. When she approved of our appearance, she would say, "*Che belle ragazze!*" (What beautiful girls!),

Figure 16   Zia Linda (author's photograph)

and seemed to absorb the mood of expectancy that we exuded. Amelio, a part owner in the shop, would occasionally mock us by calling us brutte (ugly) or particolari (strange or unique). At other times, my aunt's employees withheld their aesthetic judgements and rattled off a list of errands for us to run in the piazza. Our experiences were not unique. Older women typically inspect their nieces and daughters before they go out on the passeggiata, and their evaluations anticipated the public scrutiny that all strollers receive in this event.

Another case in point is my Aunt Linda, a sixty-nine-year-old widow who hosted me in my first six months in Sasso (figure 16). When she approved of my appearance, she would tell me, "Oggi sei bella" (Today you look good). My aunt did not approve of my penchant for baggy clothes, and when I wore jersey knit pants or loose tops she would aggressively chide me for being unfeminine and out of step with the times. During these brief exchanges, my zia (aunt) would strongly express her point of view while I would smile and quietly assert my right to wear what I chose. On these occasions, I was cast back to my teenage years in Montreal when my mother's disapproval of my taste in clothes would lead to countless squabbles. My confrontations with Zia Linda showed me how much my academic interests stemmed from my Italian immigrant culture and the emphasis that was placed on bella figura.[15]

STEPPING OUT

After the preparatory stages of the passeggiata, performers are ready to face the crowd and begin their ritual strolling. Sassani typically promenade in groups of threes or fours, and an individual will either find companions in the piazza or phone friends ahead of time to arrange a time and place to meet. On occasion people will go to the passeggiata alone with the hope of finding others with whom they can stroll. Younger people often smoke a ritual cigarette in the villa before they officially begin their promenade. While cigarette-smoking has traditionally been associated with manhood and virility, a number of young women have begun to take up this practice. A symbolic act of autonomy and sexual independence, their clandestine smoking occurs in the privacy of the villa, rather than in the home or the main thoroughfare, and serves "to pump the women up" for the public performance that is to come.

Sassani almost always enter the villa from the right and exit from the left; emerging from the villa onto the town square marks the official beginning of a stroller's promenade. (This juncture is labeled as the "threshold" point in the map of the piazza in figure 7.) Once they have crossed this point, Sassani walk past the octagonal fountain and down Corso Vittorio Emanuele with its bars, cafés, and benches filled with spectators. Passing the city hall, they reach the turning point, perform the "changing of the guard maneuver" and head back in the opposite direction. Approaching the church, Sassani may either circle the fountain and head back down *il corso* or pass again through the villa before returning for another vasca. When the event is in full swing, Corso Vittorio Emanuele is filled with an unbroken line of strolling Sassani.

Observing the townsfolk cross the threshold point, I was struck by the distinct changes that occurred in the Sassani's deportment. Here, Sassani straighten their spines and roll their shoulders back in a posture that frames their walking as a performance and acknowledges the attention of others. While strolling in the villa, the townsfolk are less likely to be aware of their environment and often walk with their gaze directed at the ground. Upon crossing the threshold point, they raised their heads and begin to take note of their social environment. As we shall see below, it is considered bad form for one to glance too obviously to the right or left while walking on the main part of *il corso*. At the threshold point, however, this stricture is relaxed. Here, Sassani are slightly elevated above the rest of *il corso* and take the opportunity to make a snapshot assessment of the action in the piazza. Swiveling their heads from left to right in a quick, almost furtive gesture, they scan the crowd and situate themselves in the flow of the promenade. These gazing techniques and changes in posture are so common that the townsfolk almost do them automatically.

Sassani use other corporeal practices to give a theatrical quality to their performance. One of these is what I call the "bodily exclamation point"; in this technique, a person talking and strolling with others can emphasize a point in the conversation by stopping abruptly and gesturing with characteristic hand motions. The power of the technique comes from the speaker's abrupt halt. If done correctly, the speaker's companions take one or two steps before recognizing that their friend has stopped and are thus forced to break their stride to pay attention to the speaker. The passeggiata indirectly trains boys and girls in the techniques of the body, and I observed children as young as six and seven using the "bodily exclamation point" in the piazza. Such stylistic flourishes add a dramatic flare to the promenade and help make the event even more entertaining for the spectators who watch attentively from afar.

Many of these bodily techniques are gender and age specific. Women, for example, often walk arm-in-arm at a moderate-to-brisk pace with their heads oriented forward and their bodies erect (figures 17–18). While eye contact is occasionally made during conversation, female participants are discouraged from turning their gaze to the right or left. This style of female comportment is the bodily enactment of the cultural proscription to *fare la strada diritta* (walk the straight path). Many of the women I interviewed remember being scolded with this biblical phrase when they walked with poor posture, strolled in a zigzag fashion, or glanced around too obtrusively during the promenade. In their recollections, correct posture was explicitly equated with good moral character, and proper strollers were deemed *retti e corretti* (literally, upright and correct) (figure 19). Most Sassani encourage their daughters to participate in the passeggiata and believe that the event instructs them in the canons of proper behavior.

A variety of forms of talk occur in the passeggiata, including lighthearted banter, teasing, and rumor. Like a catalogue of narratives, the line of parading Sassani reminds the stroller of a host of stories and gossip. For example, on one of our regular walks, my friend Cristina nonchalantly pointed out a man in the crowd who had allegedly been involved in a prostitution scandal at a local club called Twin Peaks (discussed at length in chapter 4). In an irreverent and exaggerated tone, Dina, another stroller in our group, responded by saying, "It figures, *gli mette le corna alla moglie*" (literally, to put horns on one's wife, thus making her a cuckhold). Speaking in a feminine falsetto, Riccardo, another member of the group, replied, "I wonder what his wife is going to have to say about this?" "Castration," said Dina, "like

Figure 17   Teenage women walking arm in arm (video still from the author's field tapes)

Figure 18   The forward-looking gaze (video still from the author's field tapes)

Figure 19   *Retto e corretto* (upright and correct) (video still from the author's field tapes)

that woman in America [Lorena Bobbit]." Marina countered by moving her fingers to simulate cutting scissors; "Zak, and it's finished," she said. Enjoying the silliness of my friends and egging them on, I inquired about the arrests at Twin Peaks. Cristina raised her eyebrows in a Groucho Marx fashion and said, "all the best and most respectable citizens there were paying for the services of poor, underage girls from Eastern Block countries."

The appearances of others in the promenade not only triggers gossip and banter, it also calls forth a range of aesthetic judgements. Local characters have nicknames like *la star* (a celebrity), impostato (upright and arrogant), or pancione (beer belly), and strollers constantly comment upon the gait, posture, clothing, or styles of others in the piazza. Though the aesthetic observation of others is a serious business, there exists a strong social pressure to keep the conversation in the event light-hearted and sociable. Unless there is a mutual agreement to do so, it is considered poor form to discuss serious matters at the outset of the promenade. Only after the participants have made several vasche will they begin to broach topics of any significance.

The strolling itself also has a typical rhythmic pattern. After several slow and steady laps, the walking becomes progressively faster. Some participants may break up the flow of their strolling to purchase gelato (Italian-style ice cream) or crodino (a brightly colored aperitif) or chat with spectators. The strollers control the length of these

conversations, and it is considered maleducato (impolite) for a spectator to detain a walker with too many questions. In fact, some
townsfolk prefer a completely uninterrupted passeggio (walk). The
strollers usually slow down in the final laps of the promenade, bringing
the cycle full circle and providing a smooth ending to their performance.

THE PASSEGGIATA IN SASSANO DISCOURSE

Among the residents of the surrounding towns, Sassani are well
known for their almost religious devotion to the passeggiata. At a
basic level, Sassani themselves represent the promenade as an emblem
of civic pride and a sign of their advancement into modernity. A more
careful exploration of local discourse, however, reveals a host of other
meanings. For Sassani, this site of pleasure and sensuality is both
constraining and freeing, but never value-free or monovocal. Before
looking at the different lenses through which Sassani view the passeggiata, let us briefly discuss the cultural values with which it has
become synonymous – modernity and cosmopolitanism.

As we saw in the earlier part of this chapter, Sassani like to think
of themselves as enlightened urbanites, and the terms for describing
those who succeed or fail to live up to these ideals are varied and
complex. In Sasso those who fail to be "moderno" (modern), "raffi-
nato" (refined), "civile" (civilized), *"gente che conosce il mondo esterno
ed è cosmopolita"* (people who have traveled the world and are cosmopolitan), and "aperti" (open) may be called "arretrato" (backward),
"cafone" (ignorant), "rozzo"(boorish), or outright "incivile" (uncivilized). Moderno is perhaps the most central of these concepts, tying
together a range of favorable qualities that includes education, breath
of experience, urbane sophistication, courtisiousness, and generosity.
However they position themselves in the local culture and its discourses of modernity, most townsfolk would agree that being modern
is at the heart of mainstream Sassano identity. This is what they mean
when they refer to their town as *"la piccola Parigi dell'Abruzzo"* (the
little Paris of the Abruzzo). It may seem that the Sassano rhetoric of
modernity is nothing more than a middle-class pretension to taste
and social distinction, an attempt to shed peasant roots or simply an
oppositional form of identity that the townsfolk present to outsiders
(i.e., "We are not uneducated rural folk who cling to past ways of
thinking; we are forward-looking people who welcome change.")
This collective representation, however, is more complex, and in
many ways it reveals what Sydel Silverman argues is the character-
istically urban orientation of central Italian towns (Silverman 1975). In
practice, I would suggest, individual Sassani pick and choose among
the many positive qualities associated with modernity to position

themselves within the local discourse. Working-class remigrants, for example, emphasize travel over education as the crucial modern quality, while professional women often point to their economic independence and career success as evidence of their place in modernity. While some Sassani are critical of the local discourse of modernità, no one doubts that it is central to the town's image and that the passeggiata is the place where these ideas are questioned, debated, and negotiated.

Not surprisingly, Sassani hold a wide range of opinions about the passeggiata itself. Many of the people I interviewed saw the event as a place of hedonistic amusements and modern decadence. The sensibility of the event is often characterized as *"dolce ozio"* (literally, sweet idleness or laziness). In contrast to the work ethic, the passeggiata champions the transgressive pleasures of inactivity and celebrates idle strolling as an end unto itself. Engaged in *dolce ozio*, strollers affirm the value of leisure and display their freedom from work and toil. The term *"a spasso"* (on the dole, or, literally, not working) derives from passeggiare (to be out walking) and can be used interchangeably with disoccupato (unemployed) or pigro (lazy, unproductive). At some level, Sassani fear the dangers of *dolce ozio* and social excesses associated with it – drunkenness, sexual misconduct, and political protest.

In contrast to these almost epicurean visions of the passeggiata, many Sassani see the event as repressive and coercive. In interviews and conversations, the townsfolk often complained that the oppressive scrutiny of others made the promenade into a less-than-pleasant social activity. Like Benthams' panopticon, the community polices its members through its collective gaze. Spectators sit and watch from terraces, stoops, and corners; participants judge and assess each other as they cross paths along *il corso*. Eyes scan the moving bodies to detect signs of decay and pending social faux pas. Like a hall of mirrors, the gazes of others make strollers self-conscious about their appearance and rob the event of much of its charm.[16] Sassani were only too keenly aware of being observed during the passeggiata, and many felt pressured to *di dare un buono sguardo* (to give themselves a good looking over) before stepping out into the piazza.

It is important to note that the observed can, at any moment, become the observer. Like the subject in Jean-Paul Sartre's *Being and Nothingness*, Sassani defend themselves from the objectifying gaze by turning that gaze around and objectifying others (1958, 256–68). At their worst, some Sassani make a sport of searching out other's flaws in the promenade. This is particularly worrisome because one's passeggiata performance contributes so strongly to one's public persona and reputation. While any single faux pas may be quickly forgotten in the collective memory, repeated acts of *brutta figura* (a bad face) seriously damage one's standing in the community. As a result, Sassani labor to achieve an even performance every time by walking the tight rope between spontaneity and formality to successfully accomplish the desired state of disinvoltura (naturalness, ease of manners).

In the townsfolk's most negative representation, the passeggiata is described as a "passerella" (fashion runway) – a shallow and self-aggrandizing display of Sasso's recently acquired wealth. In fact, many of the people I spoke with voiced a concern that the promenade is engendering an unhealthy emphasis on appearance and consumption. This lament is most often expressed by those in Sasso who remember the Second World War and the economic devastation that followed it. At the heart of this criticism lies a deep mistrust of modern consumer society and the greed that they believe it fosters. For example, Carmela, a seamstress in her mid-fifties, often said that Italy would be punished for its materialism and political corruption. In her apocalyptic vision, Italian society was heading for a disaster, and the residents of Sasso who had forgotten skills like subsistence farming would be caught unaware. While few Sassani predicted the social collapse that Carmela envisioned, many of the senior citizens that I spoke with mourned the postwar decline of the family economy and the artisinal trades. As we will see in chapter 3, the nationwide tangentopoli crises has only served to exacerbate the townsfolk's anxieties. While Sassani often sing the praises of technology and cheap consumer goods, the apprehension that some associate with the passeggiata is, I believe, a critique of modernity.

Despite the misgivings that the townsfolk expressed about the passeggiata, it is no less valued or praised by the community. Many Sassani with whom I spoke described their need to participate in the promenade as a hunger for human contact. Some even said that *"provano un bisogno biologico"* (they experienced a biologically drive) to go on the passeggiata, and many Sassani feel ill at ease when their routine passeggio is disrupted. This interpretation is illustrated by the experiences of another young Sassana, Pia, who studies in Rome. She said that during the semester she became jittery around five thirty in the afternoon and would feel as though a part of her was missing if she failed to go out for even a brief walk. As a ritually designated time for relaxation, the promenade allows Sassani to pursue their desire for human warmth and social contact. On an abstract level, the passeggiata represents a symbolic stance against inertia. Moving bodies, chattering voices, and theatrical displays come together to replenish the soul and break feelings of isolation. If you have had a hard day, Sassani said, the passeggiata is the "terapia" (therapy) of choice, and the townsfolk repeatedly told me they participate in the passeggiata in order to "scaricarsi" (unload), let off steam, and restore a sense of balance. In this consummate site of sociability, Sassani gather to relax, pause, and begin anew.

THE PASSEGGIATA AND MODERNITY

In the memory of the older people I interviewed, the passeggiata is always associated with the upper echelons of Italian society. During the prewar era, the event only occurred on Sunday afternoons or special religious feste (celebrations), and the peasants and artisans rarely participated. Though the promenade is still associated with wealth and elite style, the last fifty years have seen a democratization of the practice. The event now takes place seven days a week and all segments of the local society can be found strolling in the piazza. In fact, to many Sassani the passeggiata is a pubic affirmation of civic unity and community spirit. These changes are directly linked to the modernization of rural Italy, and we can get a better understanding of the contemporary passeggiata if we briefly explore the social history that formed it.

As we saw earlier, the years immediately following the Second World War saw great scarcity in Italy, while the late 1960s was a time of affluence and growth. With the modernization of the rural economy, the contadini (peasants) of the prewar period were transformed into impiegati (wage earners), and the average Sassano had more disposable income than ever before. Where the contadini may have only owned a single piece of fine clothing (the father's Sunday suit or the mother's formal dress), the impiegati of the 1970s could afford a larger wardrobe of non-work attire. The greater availability of ready-to-wear clothing, however, did not destroy the older, sartorial tradition. Many of the prewar, artisanally trained seamstresses and tailors continue to work in the town, and most Sassani have one or two handmade items in their wardrobe. Long lasting and cut to fit, these garments are among the most prized that the Sassano owns. The townsfolk also appreciate designer clothes, and there is no common agreement as to which have greater status – local hand-mades or designer originals. The cultural value placed on appearance has also paved the way for the large number of cosmeticians, hair salons, and boutiques that have emerged in the town. To the casual observer, the average Sassano of the late 1960s began to look more and more like a wealthy Italian, and, in many ways, this period was a time of cultural efflorescence.

These cultural changes correspond with the emergence of the passeggiata as Sasso's main public diversion. As their leisure time expanded and they acquired the clothes and style of the bourgeoisie, the impiegati gained access to a cultural pastime that their parents and grandparents could only observe from the sidelines. With its widened participation, the promenade became the centerpiece of the local culture. For many of today's Sassani, popular memories of social exclusion, images of bourgeois fashion, and the relative affluence of the contemporary society have combined to make the passeggiata a powerful icon of democracy and social progress.

If economic modernization has broadened Sassano participation in the promenade, then the emergence of the consumer culture and modern ideas about the individual have been equally transformative. As a number of scholars have suggested (Featherstone 1991; Hall et al. 1996), the rise of modernity has led to substantial changes in the Western notion of the self. In medieval Europe, these scholars argue, all of nature was seen as a great chain of being; determined by God and revealed by birth, the individual's social identity was a fixed part of this divine order. While medieval scholars left room for the advancement of the soul, it remained for Enlightenment thinkers to champion the notion of social mobility and democracy. With the development of consumerism, these notions of self-determination and agency were given a uniquely materialist spin. In twentieth-century capitalist discourse, individuals make and remake their identity through the consumption of commodities, and clothing and fashion are a key vehicle for this project. In Sasso, the passeggiata has become the main arena for the performance of the modern self – in both its Enlightenment and its consumerist incarnations. Although some townsfolk use the event to create the illusion of a higher class status, the passeggiata is not merely a place where the working class mascarades as the wealthy; it is also where Sassani creatively experiment with clothing and style to forge new identities and explore the meanings of gender, class, age, and generation.

But the modern self is not as protean as the ideologies of consumption would like us to believe. No matter how fresh or original, one's displays of identity are always constructed from pre-existing images and other cultural resources. Further, the crafting of the self is always informed by material limitations and concrete economic contexts. Nowhere is this clearer than in the passeggiata. Despite the fact that all members of Sassano society participate in the contemporary promenade, class differences are still keenly felt here. When Sassani viewed my videos of the passeggiata in feedback interviews, they invariably identified the townsfolk on the tape through categories that have strong class associations, such as occupation, clan name, and family affiliation. Sassani constantly comment on one another's displays, and the most common way to deflate a pompous performance is by asserting the stroller's contadini roots, for example, "*Ma quillo è de na famiglia de cafone e de pecoraio*" (Abruzzese dialect for "he comes from a family of rogues and sheep herders"). One can invoke class transcendence through fashion and style, yet in the small town of Sasso, one is always someone's daughter or son with a collectively known past. In fact, now that the passeggiata has become widely accessible, the professional and managerial classes have begun to spend their leisure time in the nearby cities of Pescara or Ancona. In their refusal to *"immedesimarsi con la folla"* (lose themselves in the crowd), they seek distinction in other places and social fora. While the contemporary passeggiata reflects the democratization of the postwar period, the event is better understood as a complex arena in which existing social relations are both challenged and affirmed.

With all of the complexity and ambivalence that Sassani feel about the passeggiata, one thing is clear: critical or celebratory, the performances that occur in the piazza are meditations on modernity. Sassani see their town as a modern one, and the passeggiata is a key place where the townsfolk openly debate and negotiate the meanings of the social changes that have come to their town in the last fifty years. By exploring this event, we not only learn about Sasso, we also see how culture informs the ways in which modernity is manifested in a particular locale and the meanings that on-the-ground actors might give to that modernity.

Of course the passeggiata is not the only place where the issue of modernity is debated. From the performances in the town's community games to the images on its postcards, much of Sassano culture is concerned with modernity, and chapters 3 and 4 will enrich our discussion by exploring how the theme of social change plays out in a wide variety of expressive forms and genres. Chapter 5 returns the discussion to the passeggiata, but before exploring Sassano culture any further, we need to examine more closely the terms and ideas which underlie the notion of "modernity." The next chapter explores the intellectual history of this concept, focusing particular attention on the relationship between modernity and culture and the vision of modernity found in traditional folklore studies. Discussing the contemporary scholarship on social change, the chapter shows how an ethnography of a small town in central Italy and the voices it presents can offer new perspectives on the problem of modernity.

2

Modernity in Folklore, Social Thought, and the Field Encounter

In the last three hundred years, the notion of modernity has been central in a wide variety of discourses. It has played a key role in academic disciplines from folklore and sociology to anthropology, cultural studies, and beyond. Not merely a scholarly construct, this notion is present in both journalistic and popular discourses throughout the West and much of the developing world. In my Sasso fieldwork I saw this theme threading itself through almost every sphere of social life.

Focusing on the relationship between modernity and culture, this chapter explores selected moments from the intellectual history of the concept of modernity to serve two main goals. On the one hand, the chapter shows how the notion of modernity informed folklore studies and adjacent disciplines. Explaining how this history shaped my research, I build on recent developments in social theory to offer new contributions to the study of expressive culture. Further, I show how contemporary methods and approaches from Mediterranean studies, reflexive ethnography, and folklore's performance school can sensitize us to the ways in which local actors make social change meaningful in their lives. Because debates about modernity extend beyond the academy, my exploration of the notion of modernity serves a second function as well, that of placing contemporary Sassano culture in its historical context. Rather than merely showing how the beliefs of on-the-ground actors have been influenced by the ideas of "great minds," the chapter reveals how the everyday thinking of Sassani can be made to speak to academic concerns and offer new perspectives on the problem of modernity.

FOLKLORE AND MODERNITY

Generally, in social theory, the term modernity refers to the wide range of changes that have occurred in Western European societies since the 1600s: industrialization, the emergence of capitalism and consumer culture, the development of the bureaucratic nation-state, and the complex transformations that have occurred in gender roles (Hall et al. 1996). Far from an anachronistic idyll, the town of Sasso displays all the features of modernity. Firmly entrenched in the contemporary money economy, the town has a manufacturing base that serves the European market and a private sector made up of small businesses and national franchises. The townsfolk are closely linked to the global community by a high-tech communications network and an efficient system of roads. Its population consists of factory workers, small-town entrepreneurs, and returning immigrants from the New World and the rest of Europe. With these changes have come a liberalization of sexual mores and an increased participation of women in the work force – although, as in North America, these changes in gender roles are a source of constant debate. In all of these ways, Sasso fits the mold of a "small town in mass society" (Vidic and Bensman 1968), and, though these changes have emerged in the recent past, Sasso conforms to the structural definition of a modern place.

The classical social theorists of the late nineteenth century described the features of modernity in terms of ideal types and evolutionary models. For Emile Durkheim, "primitive" societies display "mechanical solidarity" and tend to be homogeneous and repressive in character, while modern societies, with their greater "organic solidarity," demonstrate higher levels of specialization and interdependence (1964). Similarly, Ferdinand Tönnies (1971) believed that rational, goal-oriented gesellschaft relationships were the hallmark of modern market economies, while gemeinschaft relationships of shared identity and conviviality were characteristic of small-scale, premodern communities. The notion of conviviality is crucial for thinkers such as these. Durkheim hypothesized that the development of individualism and secularism in modern society would give rise to increasing levels of "anomie" (alienation) and discontentment. Max Weber (1968) also feared that the rationalization of tasks in industrialized society might ultimately dehumanize the individual and lead to feelings of disenchantment with the world. Articulating this distopic vision, Weber describes the modern subject as a cog in the capitalist machinery and likens modernity to an "iron cage." While Durkheim, Tönnies, and Weber never hid their criticisms of modernity, none advocated for a return to pre-industrial life.[1]

If these social philosophers embarked upon the project of under-standing modernity and modernization, then it was "folklorists [who] took up the task of comprehending traditional, pre-industrial society," explain Beverly J. Stoeltje and Richard Bauman (1989, 159). While Durkheim, Tönnies, Weber, and Marx were ambivalent about the price of social progress, they were still wedded to the rationalist ideas of the Enlightenment. Unlike these thinkers, the romantic folklorists of this period were wholeheartedly critical of contemporary social change and sought to save tradition from the onslaught of technol-ogy. Their longstanding bias against modernity has deeply influenced the development of the field and, as Bauman suggests, led many folklorists to privilege the classic notion of folk society and focus their attention on "agrarian, homogeneous, localized, face-to-face group community" (Bauman 1983, 153). In the history of the discipline, Bauman contends, there have been two responses to the decline of folk society: one has been to locate and document "relic areas" (1983, 154), and the other has been to study those realms that most clearly demonstrate "attributes that we associate with the past, namely the intimate, customary, unofficial, shared quality of interaction and com-munication conducive to conventional forms of folk expressions" (1983, 154).

The early romantic folklorists were primarily interested in docu-menting and preserving the remnants of "authentic"[2] premodern culture. For example, the eighteenth-century scholar Johann Herder (1992) believed that the soul of the German nation resided in the common lore of the people. He maintained that the spirit of the Volke could be rediscovered by studying the ancient myths, songs, and cus-toms of the unlettered peasantry. In an attempt to preserve the richness of his Anglo-Saxon heritage, the antiquarian William Thoms similarly turned to the "neglected customs" and "fading legends" of the English folk (Thoms 1965, 4). Nostalgic in his orientation, Thoms sought to reconstruct the glories of the British past by exploring how fragments of that culture survived in the games and rhymes of contemporary English children. Both Herder and Thoms espoused the romantic nationalism of their time and zealously sought to protect traditional expressive culture from the ravages of technology and modernity.

In North America, folklore began to emerge as an academic disci-pline at the turn of the twentieth century, and most of the scholars in the first fifty years of the field's academic credentializing embraced the romantic tradition. Following Herder and Thoms, they felt that mass society threatened to destroy the final remnants of the small-scale folk community. Such scholars believed that the disappearance of traditional culture would not only be a great loss for civilization, it would also mean the end of their discipline. In response to this situation, a group of folklorists whom I will call the "neoromantics" sought to reinterpret older, romantic ideas about culture and search for folklore within modernity. A complex intellectual exercise, their project was to broaden the definition of folklore without erasing the concept altogether. In practice, this meant recasting the term in more abstract ways and treating selected forms of contemporary expressive culture as folklore. Looking at the social world around them with a new optimism, the neoromantics suggested that folklore could prosper in spite of the homogenizing effects of mass society.

One dimension of this reinterpretation was to emphasize the dynamic quality of folklore. Scholars like Richard Dorson, Dell Hymes, Henry Glassie, and Barre Toelken suggested that new expressive forms could convey traditional values. They saw folklore as capable of incorporating contemporary themes and images while still maintaining its traditional essence. In the neighborhoods of urban America (Botkin 1944) or the industrial setting of Gary, Indiana (Dorson 1981), the neoromantics argued, people imaginatively reinterpreted their established repertoire of stories and folk beliefs to build and maintain small-scale communities within the modern metropolis. Henry Glassie's (1970) research on contemporary folk music, for example, showed how a codified body of expressive resources can be creatively employed by present day actors to produce songs that are both novel and traditional. Dell Hymes's often-cited presidential address to the American Folklore Society, "Folklore's Nature and the Sun's Myth" (1975), argued that there is a symbiotic relationship between tradition and innovation, continuity and change; Barre Toelken's "twin law" thesis presented similar ideas (1979).

The battle to save the romantic tradition in folklore was also fought on other fronts. Against earlier scholars who saw traditional expressive culture as an exclusively rural phenomena, Richard Dorson (1971) proclaimed that the folk could be found in the city as well as in the country. While scholars of the 1930s such as George Korson (1943, 1964) found folklore in sites of modernity like the coal mining industry, more recent occupational folklorists like Bruce McCarl (1985) and Alan Dundes (1978) discovered folk groups on the factory floor and in the office. Likewise, where past scholars bemoaned the loss of immigrant traditions, Linda Dégh (1975) and Robert Klymasz (1973) suggested that the emergent expressive culture of second- and third-generation ethnics were valid forms of folklore in their own right (see also Cicala and Stern 1991). Still other studies focused on the problem of transmission. Where past scholars felt that the mass media was opposed to folklore, Linda Dégh (1994) was one of the first folklorists to show how modern communication can serve to disseminate traditions that had been previously strictly oral, and her research urged folklorists to look at the ways in which traditional genres coexist with mass-mediated forms. Related studies sought to reveal the folk roots of popular culture, illustrating the use of traditional motifs in advertising, television, or the movies (Denby 1971; Sullenberger 1974; Mechling 1996).

While tightly focused case studies such as these worked on specific facets of the problem of folklore and modernity, seminal articles by Dan Ben-Amos (1972) and Alan Dundes (1977) sought a more abstract and general rethinking. Ben-Amos's now famous definition – folklore as "artistic communication in small groups" – unified the various threads of the then-emerging neoromantic discourse and the older equation of the agrarian, the communal, and the traditional was overturned. For a group to be a folk group, it only has to generate expressive culture and exist on a small scale – although, for Ben-Amos, these modern small groups still tend to retain the intimacy, homogeneity, and conviviality of Tönnies's gemeinschaft communities. Dundes's statement was even broader, allowing the folk group to be based on even a single feature of shared identity and to exist on both the large- and the small-scale. Though the neoromantics problematized the relationship between folklore and high or mass culture (and though they highlighted the interplay between folk, elite, and mass), they still sought to maintain the integrity of these categories. The key point here is that, for most of these scholars, folklore is still opposed to the modern, but modernity (manifested as rapid social change, urbanization, and mass culture) is not able to quash the humane expressive forms of the small-scale community unified by a common identity.

If the original romantics saw a strong opposition between tradition and modernity, the neoromantics sought to allow tradition and modernity to coexist without either losing its integrity. Here, modernity and tradition are seen as being locked in a controlled dialectic that varies, but never consumes or redefines, its poles. This work was an important step forward for the field, but this solution produces its own set of problems. These can be best illustrated by exploring the work of a scholar who took a very different approach to the relationship between culture and modernity – anthropologist Milton Singer. Unlike the programmatic work of most neoromantic theorists, Singer treats the concepts of tradition and modernity as phenomena whose nature is to be discovered in the field and reveals the ways in which these forces are experienced in the everyday life of his informants. Foreshadowing many of the most recent developments in social and cultural theory, his work on social change in India is highly instructive.

In his classic ethnography *When a Great Tradition Modernizes* (1972), Singer explores the adaptive mechanisms by which Indians incorporate innovation in their lives and reinterpret traditional practices for secular ends. In so doing, he shows how the processes of "traditionalization" and "modernization" are inextricably linked with one another. Though it is not explicitly stated in the text, Singer suggests that only some of the possible relationships between tradition and modernity are realized in any given culture. While there is an emphasis on "traditionalization" in Singer's India, other societies, he implies, may embody different dialectics. A dynamic and flexible system of beliefs, traditionalizing Hinduism transforms and co-opts modern influences, making the new old. Hence, the sari made with nylon fiber is still traditional and the Brahmin businessman who fails to worship at the temple is still a believer and has not broken any Sanskrit law. Where the neoromantics conceptualized folklore as an isolatable set of cultural dynamics opposed to – but not quashed by – modernity, Singer sees a wide range of dialectics between tradition and modernity. For him, modernity and tradition may be both conflictual and symbiotic, antagonistic and complimentary. Further, where the neoromantics view folklore's incorporation of the modern as the necessary resistance of the folk to alienation, Singer sees Hinduism's incorporation of modernity as a culturally specific ideology of historical change.

One of the main goals of this study is to build upon Singer's work and reveal other ways that the dialectics of tradition and modernity play themselves out in culture. If modernization in Indian society is subsumed under the category of tradition, Sassani in their passeggiata profess a rhetoric of perpetual modernity: we are enlightened, urban, up-to-date, and always changing, their performances say. Unlike the residents of Madras, the townsfolk of Sasso embrace the values of cosmopolitaness and publically proclaim their avid commitment to what is new and progressive. In short, for today's Sassani, modernity is the tradition.

Within folklore, a number of scholars have explored related dialectics of tradition and modernity and provided a critique of the romantic association between folklore and conviviality, gemeinschaft, or shared identity. These scholars reveal that folklore is not always produced in small groups or created in the service of tradition. Richard Bauman's concept of differential identity (1972) speaks directly to this issue by drawing attention to the expressive culture which emerges *between* rather than within groups. Likewise, scholars of community events have shown that public enactments are not only expressions of communal solidarity, but of ideological conflict and political dissent (Manning 1989; Magliocco 1993). And while scholars have long taken folklore as an expression of tradition, the work of Stoeltje and Bauman (1989) has shown that events such as festivals or parades may primarily concern themselves with the meanings of modernity.

Like romanticism before it, neoromantic folklore is important because it serves as a corrective to humanities scholarship that privileges elite culture or to any research that ignores the role of expressive behavior in society. The difficulty is that, while neoromanticism has emphasized the interplay between mass and folk, this orientation still treats folklore (the stuff) as a discrete category of culture, and folklore (the discipline) as the study of those materials. If we want to understand the complex, historically emergent lives of the people with whom we work, we cannot allow a priori theoretical conceptions to restrict our choice of study objects. This is not to say that traditional folklore is either irrelevant or moribund, but to emphasize two points. First, the types of expressive culture (mass culture, folk culture, high culture) and their social bases (mass society, folk community, elite circles) are essentially emergent, and history produces new social structures and expressive forms that will continually confound the classic nineteenth-century social theoretic categories. Second, expressive forms don't necessarily operate in the way that highly ideological theory suggests (i.e., folklore does not necessarily contribute to the maintenance of gemeinschaft communities; mass culture is not necessarily a homogenizing or repressive force, and so forth).

At their best, the classical nineteenth-century definitions of folklore described a historically specific set of expressive forms and their attendant social relations. There is good reason to believe, however, that the constellation of features that these writers emphasized – the small scale, the convivial, the gemeinschaft, the traditional – are highly idealized (Bauman 1983). Even though the expanded definitions of the neoromantic folklorists (Ben-Amos 1972; Dundes 1977) helped overcome past ideological problems, there is no reason to assume that even their expanded vision – Ben Amos's "artistic communication in small groups" – is universal, necessary, or transhistorical. While "artistic communication in small groups" clearly occurs, students of folklore must resist the urge to naturalize folklore and only focus on face-to-face communication. Neither should we restrict ourselves to seeking out the linkages between "folklore" and other forms – finding, for example, traditional legend motifs in television advertising. Perhaps what is most important is that we must avoid the pitfall of folklorizing the modern and restricting our view of popular culture to only those forms that display traditionally folkloric dynamics (i.e., the gemeinschaft communities of youth subcultures or the collaborative, "folklike" compositional processes that occur in the entertainment industry). Instead, we should focus on the issues and themes that concern the people we study and attend to the unique modes of communications that exist in the society in which they live – regardless of how well or poorly that communication conforms to pre-existing theoretical models. And while we may find stereotypically folkloric folklore (or folkloric dynamics within mass culture), we must be on the lookout for new cultural forms that evade these typologies altogether.

Some examples from my fieldwork will help to illustrate these ideas. Before I left for Italy, I knew that I wanted to study both face-to-face interactions and mass-mediated genres, and that I didn't want to make assumptions about the character of expressive life in Sasso. From an ethnographic perspective, I also sought to attend to forms of communication that fell between the analytic cracks of my discipline. In the first stages of my fieldwork, casual conversation and everyday experience led me to the themes in Sassano society that became central to this study: cosmopolitanism and local identity, changing gender roles, industrialization, class tensions, and the problems of the bureaucratic state. I knew that these themes were related, but it was only later that I realized that they were all tied to the question of modernity. Following my nose, I allowed the themes to guide me to different research pathways and domains of expressive culture.

During my time in Sasso a number of important cultural phenomena occurred on the local and national scene and occupied the interest of the townsfolk. In 1994 Ylenia Carrisi, the daughter of the famous Italian singing couple Al Bano and Romina Power, disappeared in New Orleans. This event generated a great deal of media hype and spawned many lively conversations in Sasso. As I listened to people make impromptu remarks about the young woman's honor and integrity, I realized that the Ylenia case was a collective Rorschach for understanding Sassano attitudes about gender. The scandal of Twin Peaks, a local discotheque that was shut down because of drugs and prostitution, also stirred controversy in the community, and the discussion that surrounded this affair proved itself to be a fascinating, multilayered dialogue about regional others, the price of progress, and the corrupting influence of wealth in Sasso. Similarly, the community games, *Giochi Senza Frontiere* (Games Without Frontiers), which were inspired by a television show, provided an arena in which Sassani reflected upon and debated the issues of modernity and local identity.

Each one of these examples confounds simple definitions of mass and folk culture. The popular discourse surrounding the Carrisi disappearance ties Italy to the United States, and, in analyzing this affair in chapter 4, I explore representations from the national television and regional newspapers as well as local, on-the-ground perspectives. The Twin Peaks scandal was a local event, but the issues of regional identity and changing gender roles that it unearths are ones characteristic of modernity, not tradition. Similarly, the community games were inspired by a television show popular throughout Europe, and my analysis reveals how the games serve as a whimsical collective meditation on social change.

Exploring the representation of Sasso in the national mass media, I found yet another set of cultural dynamics. When I arrived in 1993, the tangentopoli (literally, bribesville; a political imbroglio that involved systematic abuses at the highest levels of the Italian government) crisis was at a fever pitch. Both local and provincial politicians were implicated in this national scandal. Sasso's mayor and a number of town officials were being investigated for graft, and the executive council of the Abruzzo had been fired for mismanaging European development funds. Over the next few weeks, Sassani repeatedly told me that I should watch a recent episode of L'Istruttoria (literally, court hearing; a national television news magazine), which investigated the corruption in Sasso. Using L'Istruttoria as a point of departure, my conversations with the townsfolk revealed local ideas about class, development, political corruption in the bureaucratic state, and Sassano identity. Here, mass media representations and local reception operate much as traditional folklore theory predicts they might: the mass media depicts the locals as "backward" primitives, while the local, "folk" response critiques the national representations and depicts modernity as the source of declining public ethics.

Other expressive forms, however, did not fit traditional theory so neatly. During my fieldwork, the Argentinean soap opera Milagros was extremely popular with some segments of Sassano society. In conventional romantic folkloristics, mass entertainment is believed to degrade small-scale cultures, make the local lose its unique character, and foster social change. In contrast, Milagros spoke to the most traditional visions of gender in Sasso and was avidly viewed by the town's most conservative group – older, working-class women. Employing traditional Catholic imagery and depicting women as the guardians of sexual virtue, Milagros is part of a distinctively pan-Catholic media culture that unites widely dispersed localities in Latin America and the Mediterranean. More ironic for conventional folklore theory, it is this mass-mediated form, not some genre of local folk narrative, that most strongly articulates and reinforces traditional ideas about gender and sexuality. In chapter 4, I examine how older, female viewers use *Milagros* to make sense of their marginalized role in the town and its changing gender relations.

While no one from Sasso directly led me to the postcards that I discuss in chapter 3, I include them because they provide a good point of comparison with the passeggiata and the national tourist literature. All three bodies of data provide public statements on modernity and the character of life in Sasso. But while the passeggiata might be summarily characterized as a folk custom or festival, the postcards cannot be so easily categorized. Though they are sold commercially, the postcards are created neither to serve a mass market nor to fulfill the profit motive. Though they are locally produced, their intended audience is not the townsfolk themselves but the small group of Sassani who have immigrated to other countries and have returned to the town for a vacation. Produced by one segment of the local society, purchased by visiting expatriates, and consumed by hyphenated ethnics in the New World, the postcards confound the classic definitions of mass and folk culture. The postcards serve as platform for the representation of Sasso by the town's elite, and, unlike the conflicting perspectives found in the passeggiata, the postcards uniformly depict the town as a harmonious blend of tradition and modernity. Taken together, the national tourist literature, the postcards, and the passeggiata operate as a complex discourse about regional and local identity.

The passeggiata is yet another example of an expressive form that defies neoromantic ideas about folklore and modernity. While the Italian passeggiata is often represented as a timeless Mediterranean pastime – indeed one can find references to some type of promenading at least as far back as Petrarca – the passeggiata in its contemporary form has only risen to prominence since the nineteenth century. The emergence of inexpensive consumer goods and the rise of the impiegati (waged earner) in the postwar period have been the main forces for ushering the passeggiata into the center of Sasso's cultural life. In romantic folklore, customs of this kind are often viewed as a locus of tradition and an affirmation of collective identity. While some traditional beliefs are displayed in the passeggiata, it would be a mistake to see the event as nothing more than a modern expression of traditional values. Rife with social tensions, the passeggiata is used by Sassani to interpret and debate the virtues of industrialization, changing gender roles, and the problems of political strife and generational conflict. In short, the passeggiata is about the meaning of modernity; it is neither concerned with maintaining tradition nor mourning its loss. The self-avowed moderns of *"la piccola Parigi dell'Abruzzo"* view the passeggiata as an icon of their cosmopolitaness. If they see it as traditional at all, the passeggiata represents the tradition of urbane sophistication and style so highly valued by the residents.

"MULTIPLE MODERNITIES" AND GLOBALIZATION IN CONTEMPORARY SOCIAL THEORY

In recent social theory older notions of modernity have been subjected to sustained critical scrutiny, and this contemporary scholarship is highly relevant to our topic. Though there is substantial diversity in the thought of today's writers, many find common ground in their rejection of 1950s and 1960s ideas about modernization, often dubbed "convergence theories" (Parsons 1951; Rostow 1960). This work posited a unilinear theory of development from traditional societies to modern ones. Technology is seen here as a universal social good, and the advancement of technology would inevitably lead to a remaking of "primitive cultures" in which reason and individual rights would triumph over superstition and the iron hand of established authority. Implicit in all of this is that Western Europe and the United States will lead the world in modernization, and that liberal democracy and the cultural style of these countries will be the template for all future societies. As philosopher Charles Taylor aptly points out, this paradigm reduces social change to technological change and makes modern social values synonymous with Enlightenment values (Taylor 1999). In thinking that increased secularization and individualism are the necessary conditions of modernity, Taylor argues, the convergence theorists not only imposed a falsely uniform pattern of change on non-Western cultures, they also obscured how those societies may integrate or reinterpret features of modern Western culture.

In contrast to convergence theory, many contemporary thinkers suggest that multiple forms of modernity may exist and that these may surface in differing places and times. Rather than treating technology as the engine driving social and cultural change, these so-called "alternative (or multiple) modernity theorists" argue that the same forms of technology may impact different societies in different ways. Further, these scholars see social change as the outcome of numerous forces, among them historical, cultural, or religious phenomena pre-existing in a given locale. For example, writing in the journal *Public Culture*, rhetoric scholar Dilip Parameshwar Gaonkar

(1999) argues that modernity always unfolds within a specific cultural context and that differing starting points for the transition to modernity lead to differing outcomes. Likewise, Taylor maintains that a Japanese modernity, an Indian modernity, or an Islamic modernity are no more defined by their rejection of tradition than they are mere imitations of the West (1999). "The realm of 'tradition' and 'custom' offers much of the symbolic material around which local communities, interested groups, and classes rework and refashion the modernizations of capitalist transformations," argues cultural geographer Michael John Watts (1992, 15). While alternate modernities are often fashioned from Western modernities, they are not taken on whole cloth to the exclusion of local belief. To the contrary, societies afraid of compromising their indigenous culture to Western ideology may exercise a kind of resistance by setting foreign technological innovations to the service of local cultural needs (Taylor 1999).

An important part of the current debate centers around the tendency in both the social sciences and in the humanities to conceive of modernity temporally instead of spatially. Recent work in the fields of political science, (Wittrock 2000), sociology (Eisenstadt 2000), and cultural geography (Pred and Watts 1992) all suggest that viewing modernity as part of a homogeneous historical period with an underlying set of social structural features neglects the fact that modernity is lived in different ways by different peoples with different cultures and histories. These researchers are calling for a theory of modernity leavened by rich empirical data and for a style of scholarship that tacks back and forth between the conceptual and the concrete. Such work, the multiple modernity theorists argue, must take into account how historically situated actors map out the differing meanings of social change in various cultural contexts. For example, in *Reworking Modernity*, Watts argues that theorists have neglected "people, communities, networks, and struggles; in short, the socially differentiated experiences of, and responses to globalization" and modernization (1992, 14). "There is little in the way of ethnography [in the modernity literature]," he argues, "and hence ... equally little in the way of palpable experience, of how literally millions of people struggle to handle, deal with, represent, and interpret the Galactic metropolis" – the transformations brought on by the proliferation of modernity to diverse world cultures (Watts 1992, 14).

In many ways, my work seeks to carry forth the project of the multiple modernity theorists. Responding to the call for ethnographically grounded studies of modernity in diverse geographical locations, this study shows how industrialization and its related phenomena have shaped small-town life in central Italy. But rather than viewing modernization as a cross-culturally uniform process, I see historical change as the outcome of both structural forces and the contingent efforts of situated actors. By exploring what Singer has called "cultural performance" (1972), this study examines the complex, polyphonic discourses through which actors of various social positions reflect upon and debate the meanings of the very modernity they themselves are creating. Exploring the on-the-ground lived experiences of social change in a specific locale, I hope to illuminate the symbolic resources and expressive forms people use to question, negotiate, and fashion modernity in both everyday conversation and mundane social practices. And like the multiple modernities theorists, my study seeks to move away from more romantic approaches to social change that only register nostalgia and loss in the contemporary world. Against this older view, my work reveals how the premodern and modern exist together, not only in material conditions but in philosophy and outlook. In the Sassano economy, for example, the presence of European multinational corporations operates alongside an informal barter economy; likewise in the cultural sphere, Sassani will move from traditional pastimes like passeggiata-strolling, small-scale farming, and winemaking to the consumption of transnational media products and imported designer fashions. And in their public ruminations on the meaning of modernity, Sassani express a broad range of perspectives, from a full-blown celebration of modernity, to a wistful longing for the past, to a sharper dissatisfaction with social change, to more conflicted and ambivalent attitudes.

In registering Sassano discourse about modernity, this study engages another academic literature. One of the reasons that modernity is so difficult to talk about is that the term is given different meanings in different intellectual contexts. If the controversy over convergence theory revolves around the question of whether or not modernity exists as a universal stage of historical development, a parallel but distinct strand of discourse – what Gaonkar calls "cultural modernity" (1999, 2) – accepts the existence of modernity as a historical period and instead debates the meaning and value of that period. The classical nineteenth-century social theorists discussed above participated in both of these intellectual streams, both defining modernity as a unique set of social transformations and assessing the impact of those transformations on the human condition. But, if the classical theorists tended to be ambivalent about the value of modernity, many writers and artists in the eighteenth and nineteenth centuries were more pessimistic. Like the nineteenth-century folklorists explored above, literary figures of the romantic tradition interpreted the social changes of modernity through a narrative of degradation and loss; they looked to an idealized vision of the medieval period as an artistic golden age. Similarly disparaging of modernity but oriented toward the future, avant-garde belle-lettreists criticized what they saw as the new "middle-class ethos" of conformity, pragmatism, and acquisitiveness and sought to overcome the oppressive homogenization of modernity by cultivating individuality, creativity, and artistic self-expression (Gaonkar 1999).

It is not, I argue, only "great minds" who reflect upon the meaning of modernity; on-the-ground actors explore and discuss these ideas as well, and this study seeks to bring Sassano popular debates about modernity to a wider audience. With these goals in mind I view my fieldwork not so much as a "giving of voice" to the voiceless victims of modernity – for Sassani are anything but quiet – but as offering an ethnographic microphone for capturing the rich conversations that emerge in Sassano cultural performance. While it would be naive to think that Sassani have been uninfluenced by the long history of academic and artistic musings about the meaning of modernity, it would be equally in error to think that ordinary people merely reflect and reproduce the ideas of the "great thinkers" of the past.

As I have suggested, the discourse about modernity in Sasso is highly multivocal. If, however, there is a local consensus on this topic, it is that, while modernity has its problems, it is to be embraced and ultimately redeemed through aesthetic fulfillment. Here, Sassani maintain a position similar to that held by Charles Baudelaire, who, as Gaonkar observes, felt that life under conditions of modernity could only be made meaningful by turning it into an object of beauty and contemplation. What is perhaps most interesting is that Sassani and Baudelaire alike recognize the poetic value of the spectacle of public life and the refined skills of observation that one must cultivate in order to grasp the moments of "eternity" that exist in the flux of everyday experience (on Baudelaire's view of modernity, see Gaonkar 1999).

While in this project I use my ethnographic research on Italy to carry forward the multiple modernities program, I also wish to suggest new approaches to the underlying theoretical debate. Certainly the multiple modernities theorists set themselves in opposition to convergence theory. Exploring the contemporary literature, however, I prefer to see the difference between these theories as one of emphasis rather than essence. If the analysis of the multiple modernities theorists foreground the difference between contemporary Hindu India, Muslim Indonesia, and the Christian West, they nevertheless implicitly assume that there are at least some features that are shared by all of these societies and serve to define them as "modern." In other words, for social thinkers to theorize the existence of multiple modernities, they must implicitly assume a set of core characteristics that makes these multiple variants all "modern." If this were not the case, on what grounds would we be justified in excluding any society

– eleventh-century China or the Shona of the fourteenth century – from an analysis of the varieties of modernity? Unstated but suggested by this literature is a traditional base and superstructure argument – that modern societies are those with at least a modicum of industrialization and perhaps urbanization and national bureaucratic structures. Rethinking the multiple modernities critique, I argue that we as theorist must be more explicit about what it is that would qualify a society as modern. Rather than merely looking at the multiple forms of modernity, we should orient our historical and ethnographic comparison toward a search for correlations, or tendencies for correlation, between those features that have been traditionally associated with modernity. Clearly, industrialization does not necessarily result in secularization, but does it necessitate the emergence of new, individualistic identities? How much variability is there in the relationship between changing gender roles, the mass media, the growth of the nation-state, and cultural homogeneity? A more robust theory will yoke the emerging ethnographies of modernity together to separate the necessary features of modernity from the contingent ones and reveal which social and cultural features tend to co-occur and which oppose one another.

Related to, but distinct from, modernity theory is the scholarly literature that has emerged around the term "globalization." While an extensive discussion of these writings is beyond the scope of this study, it will be worthwhile to briefly explore the points of contact between these bodies of work. In its broadest sense, the term globalization refers to the emergence of social processes that flow across national borders and large areas of space; such phenomena tend to blur the boundaries between individual societies and lead to greater economic, political, and cultural interdependence. Anthropologist Jonathan Friedman (1995) explains that within the context of globalization, the "rate of transportation of people, sound, pictures [and the] accumulation of capital" proliferate with an ever-increasing speed and intensity (70), a process that David Harvey refers to as "time-space compression" (2000). Some theorists, such as Anthony Giddens (1990), see globalization as the outcome of modernity in the West. Others see it, not as a product of Western modernity and its colonialist or postcolonialist expansion, but as a broader phenomenon of worldwide socioeconomic integration. Like modernity, globalization is also frequently linked with an enhanced awareness of global others and a heightened reflexive consciousness (Giddens 1990; Hannerz 1990; Robertson 1995; Harvey 2000). Giddens states that in globalization there is an "intensification of worldwide social relations which link distant localities in such a way as local happenings are shaped by events occurring many miles away and vice versa" (Giddens

1990, 64). With the rise of globalization in Southeast Asia and the United States, for example, the affluence of a neighborhood in Singapore, Giddens explains, can only be truly understood within the context of the impoverishment of a neighborhood in Pittsburgh (Giddens 1990).

As in the multiple modernities literature, a growing number of globalization theorists have urged scholars to pay greater attention to the differing ways in which global processes unfold in particular locales and, as Janet Wolff argues (1997), for theory to be more richly informed by ethnographic data. Anthropologist Arjun Appadurai, for example, has criticized scholars who, largely on theoretical grounds, equate globalization with cultural homogenization. Updating the fears of social uniformity expressed by past critics of modernity, early globalization theorists were concerned that the spread of social processes across large stretches of space would lead to a planetary cultural "gray out." More recently, however, scholars have emphasized that globalization may also be associated with the presence of increased cultural *difference*. Appadurai observes that the critique of cultural homogenization often devolves into "an argument about Americanization or an argument about commoditization, and very often the two arguments are closely linked" (Appadurai 1996, 32). What this perspective fails to understand, he contends, is that the social practices and cultural forms that are introduced into new societies are rapidly "indigenized" (combined with local practices and forms to produce uniquely local hybrids), and Appadurai illustrates how the models of push and pull found in migration studies or neo-Marxist theories of consumer/producer relations in economic development are far too simple for understanding the uneven and contradictory ways in which global capitalism operates. Rather than allowing ourselves to be content with the common wisdom of development theory and the cases that most readily conform to it, we must, Appadurai argues, attend to the diverse and irregular ways in which societies engage with globalizing forces. By exploring what he sees as the five dimensions of social life under conditions of globalization ("ethnoscapes," "mediascapes," "technoscapes," "financescapes," and "ideoscapes"), Appadurai believes we can begin to find patterns in the differing ways in which globalization is expressed in various cultural settings (Appadurai 1996). Central to any such analysis must be a sensitivity to the issue of power. As Mike Featherstone explains, "various agencies, institutions, and interest groups will seek to manipulate, channel (close or open up) the cultural boundaries of others to … [global] flows" (Featherstone 1990, 7).

Exploring different aspects of the problem, social anthropologist Ulf Hannerz (1997) also finds fault with earlier work on globalization, which he sees as largely divided between theories of "cultural homogenization" and theories of "peripheral corruption." In the former, the diversity of local folk cultures are represented as being slowly eroded by the encroaching threat of Western hegemony. The later takes a different view, criticizing peripheral Third World localities for adopting Western technology but failing to assimilate the Enlightenment principles of reason, individual rights, and liberal democracy, which they believe should accompany it (Hannerz 1997). Hannerz maintains that we must get beyond these dichotomies and explore the complex ways in which the local and the global interact with one another in specific situations. Echoing similar concerns, sociologist Janet Abu-Lughod challenges us to discover in our field sites "exactly just what [local social process or cultural form] is syncretizing [i.e., being combined with external processes or forms to produce a unique local hybrid], what is globalizing [being drawn into a homogeneous global culture], and what remains unconvergent in our so called global village" (Abu-Lughod 1996, 134). Considering the interpretation of cultural artifacts, for example, Abu-Lughod emphasizes that, while individual items of expressive culture may get homogenized in global circulation, they may be received differently by members of differing ethnic groups and may even be read differently by differing segments within a single ethnicity. By discussing the complex politics that surround the reception of Salman Rushdie's book *The Satanic Verses*, Abu-Lughod effectively shows how this text speaks to cosmopolitan bilingual Muslims in England and ethnically English audiences in diametrically opposed ways. While the former group of readers are familiar with the cultural allusions of *The Satanic Verses* but finds its content offensive, the later recognize that the book is somewhat ironic but do not fully comprehend the references (Abu-Lughod 1996). To Abu-Lughod's reading, the Rushdie incident reveals how a single country may display both globalized and unglobalized tendencies.

Building upon the work of Appadurai, Hannerz, and Abu-Lughod, my study of Sasso explores a unique set of global dynamics in a particular locale. In the financescape, the national and transnational blur as development funds from both Rome, the center of the Italian national government, and Brussels, the home of the European Community, flow into local coffers. Further, the local and global economies intersect – or, in the language of the modernity literature, modern economic practices are traditionalized – as wage laborers augment the income from their factory jobs with goods from the family economy and the system of local bartering. Shifting from financescapes to mediascapes, we see a different set of local/global dynamics in the Sassano reception of television and newspapers. Rather than producing cultural gray out, the Latin American telenovelas (soap operas) that are beamed into Sassano homes vividly speak to older, working class homemakers who do not readily identify with the culture of contemporary Italy. Here, the transnational media fosters traditional, rather than modern, values and welds together the disparate Catholic communities that pre-information-age colonialism had scattered across the world. By comparing these examples, I suggest, we can see the complex and often contradictory ways in which situated actors envision their relationship to localities and larger social formations. In the financescape, Sassano perspectives blur Rome and Brussels together into a single category – a bureaucratic other that is seen either as a source of progress and development, or, alternately, as a corrupting force for modernization. In the mediascape, however, selected local constituencies form collegial alliances across vast areas to construct a pan-Catholic identity. Clearly, globalization is a divergent and uneven process, and the Sassano data suggest that the actors' interpretations of such phenomena are no less complex.

Though the passeggiata is a traditional expressive practice carried out in face-to-face interactions, it too is caught up with issues of globalization. The event is saturated with images from the local, the national, and the transnational. Seeking to evoke airs of worldliness, for example, teenage women affect the poses and styles of European fashion magazines. In everyday conversations the townsfolk point to the passeggiata as evidence of their cosmopolitan nature. Further, a backgrounded awareness of the fact that the residents of Sasso represent the portion of the population that resisted the lure of outmigration informs much of the local identity and the displays of style that take place in the town's piazza. Performing their divergent visions of what it means to live in "Our Little Paris," the townsfolk explore the relationships between Sasso and Italy, Sasso and Europe, and Sasso and the countries of the more distant outmigration – Canada, the United States, Argentina, Venezuela, and Australia. To understand the issues of globalization and culture, I suggest, requires that we as students of culture display greater interpretative sensitivity not only to the social processes that bind or separate the local and the global but also to the meanings that on-the-ground actors find in those processes. While unproblematic examples of homogenization (Schiller 1985), cultural imperialism (Tomalison 1991), hybrid cultural blending (Pieterse 1995; Hannerz 1987), and the resistant local co-optation of consumer commodities (Fabian 1978; Barber 1987; Friedman 1990) can be found in the ethnographic literature, many situations aren't so clear cut. In a festival-like sphere of interaction such as the passeggiata – with its multiple and simultaneous performances, multiple actors, and multiple interpretation – it is to be expected that a range of relationships between the local and the global will be articulated. Advancing the work of Appadurai, Hannerz, and Abu-Lughod, I seek to go beyond the arguments that simplistically decry cultural loss[3] or too easily celebrate creative hybridity and instead explore the complex ways in which passeggiata participants position themselves in relation to identities of various scales and types. While this study is mainly grounded in the theoretical literature on modernity, I hope my work will shed new light on the interplay of the local and the global and speak to the interests of globalization scholars.

PERFORMANCE, STYLE, AND THE BODY

The theoretical work on modernity and folklore posits a relationship between particular kinds of societies and the character and meaning of the expressive culture that they engender. Emphasizing the social functions of the mass media and the role that artistic communication plays in small groups, such work tends to focus less attention on the concrete practices by which folklore is created and interpreted. While this study uses the passeggiata and other cultural forms to shed light on the larger problem of modernity, it is also concerned with expressive practices in their own right – particular acts or broader styles of grooming, applying makeup, dressing, choosing accessories, strolling, gesturing, and greeting. Because of the nature of central Italian social and aesthetic ideologies, the analysis of expressive practices themselves must be made front and center of any study of modernity in Sasso, and this is true for two reasons. On a basic level, the people with whom I did my research are deeply concerned with acquiring and honing their expressive skills; because of this alone expressive practices would call out for our attention. But perhaps more important, Sassani feel that modernity is as much about urbane aesthetics as it is about industrialization or changing gender roles, and the development of artistic resources is a key part of that aesthetic. If we are to gain deeper insights into Sassano perspectives on modernity, we must explore in detail the expressive practices that occur in the town.

Erving Goffman and Folklore's Performance School

My fascination with appearance, clothes, and public decorum is rooted in my Italian immigrant upbringing. As the daughter of a talented seamstress trained in *l'arte di cucire* (the art of sewing), my mother, a native of Sasso, had strong views about the aesthetics of clothing. At an early age, I discovered that certain people excelled at cutting *una bella figura*, while others were less gifted in achieving the desired effect. As a woman I felt special pressure to master the skills of appearance and comportment and to learn the secret rules of feminine poise. In the ethnic enclave of St Michel in Montreal, I was intrigued by my family's elaborate system of aesthetics. At school, church, and social occasions the Italian immigrants of my community all had strong ideas about *il bello* (the pretty) or *il brutto* (the ugly). During any social interaction there was always a great deal of discussioni (verbal debates) about the aesthetic and sensual dimensions of food, dress, and manners. These issues and concerns originally drew me to the field of sociology and the work of Erving Goffman. Later, as a doctoral student, I was intrigued by the work of performance-oriented folklore scholars and their exploration of artistic behavior around the world.

Goffman's path-breaking research on the presentation of self (1959, 1961, 1967, 1983) provides a key theoretical framework for the analysis of everyday expressive practices. The consummate social analyst, Goffman shows how people creatively control their behavior in mundane interactions to manage the impressions they create. His work not only reveals the means by which interaction is achieved (gesture, language use, facial expression), he also shows that interaction is *strategic* (1972) – that is, situated within a social context of norms and rules and creatively deployed to achieve social ends. In his emphasis on both the pre-given character of social roles and the creative ways in which people manipulate those roles, Goffman's orientation has important affinities with the contemporary concern for agency in social life. Perhaps most important for this study, Goffman's emphasis on the strategic and the pragmatic dimensions of interaction informed performance theory's interest in rhetoric and the social uses of folklore. While Goffman's work is theoretically suggestive, many of his ideas are not fully fleshed out in field research, and one of the goals of this study is to ground Goffman's somewhat elusive concept of impression management (1959) in concrete ethnographic data. Further, Goffman's insights in this area are crucial because they reveal the mechanisms by which the presentation and interpretation of self operate.

Another dimension of Goffman's work is his emphasis on the importance of situated conduct for macro-social phenomena. In his 1983 Presidential Address to the American Sociological Society, Goffman suggested that face-to-face interaction is the site where institutional power and agentive choice vie for control. It is in such events that we can discover what abstract social theoretic concepts such as struggle, influence, and resistance mean in concrete experiences and how they play themselves out in the practices of people's lives; here, we see how behaviors are regulated by normative values but never fully contained by them. Goffman's emphasis on the informal and less routinized forms of interaction is consonant with folklore's longstanding interest in non-elite culture and quotidian expressive practices. Building on this tradition, I hope to show how individuals respond to, reproduce, and resist larger social forces like modernization and development.[4]

Informed by Goffman, performance-oriented scholars in folklore have shown how people use everyday expressive culture to negotiate issues of status, identity, and power in different situations (Abrahams 1968, 1970, 1975; Kirshenblatt-Gimblett 1972; Bauman 1977; Babcock 1978; Briggs 1988; Berger and Del Negro 2004). For example, Roger Abrahams's research illustrates the ways men and women artfully manipulate language in expressive behavior to accomplish social goals. In his seminal "Introductory Remarks to a Rhetorical Theory of Folklore"(1968), Abrahams discusses how people in different cultures employ folklore as a tool of persuasion and influence. In more contemporary research, scholars have focused on reflexive language and shown how performers use subtle features of linguistic structure to enhance the rhetorical effect of situated verbal performance (Kratz 1990; Parmentier 1993; Soloman 1994). What is most important here is the idea that folklore is not solely an aesthetic statement but can also be a pragmatic response to individual needs or the pressures of social change. This touchstone concept in performance theory has shaped my thinking about Sassano culture. Discussing the passeggiata in chapters 5 and 6, I show how performances of urbane sophistication are used by the townsfolk to carve a niche for themselves in the local society and suggest the role that the idea of aesthetics plays in local discourse on modernity.

The concepts of skill and accountability that Richard Bauman outlines in *Verbal Art as Performance* (1977) have been particularly useful in helping me to think about public display in Sassano culture. To more fully comprehend the indigenous aesthetic criteria that underlie the passeggiata, I videotaped the event, viewed the tapes with the townsfolk, and conducted feedback interviews. Here, the notions of disinvoltura and *bella figura* emerged as culturally specific standards for judging performance. Led by Bauman's analysis, I came to realize that such standards serve additional functions as well. In the local belief system, bodily displays are seen as an indicator of moral character, and my analysis shows how good performance is interpreted as a sign of integrity and bad performance is seen as an indicator of dishonesty or disrespect for the community. In a place where aesthetic display is held in high regard and tied to broader cultural values, artistic accountability becomes a larger sign of moral accountability.

Another dimension of the performance studies project is a concern for the event as a unit of analysis. A reaction against older, text-based research, performance scholars stressed that we must take the social situation as a whole, rather than discrete items or genres, as our study object. While a number of folklorists have explored costume (Yoder 1972; Wilson 1996) and kinesics (Fine 1984; Kapchan 1994), the majority of performance-oriented studies in folklore still focus on language. Exploring clothing, gesture, gait, comportment, and facial expressions in the passeggiata, I hope to focus greater attention on the nonlinguistic behavior in the performance event and highlight the ways in which the various dimensions of communication inform and interact with one another in the expressive act.

The similarities and differences between the work of Erving Goffman and that of the performance school are important and suggestive. Both bodies of literature are concerned with the techniques by which social interaction is achieved and the larger goals that those techniques are used to serve. The difference between their approaches lies in emphasis, and the situation is highly ironic. Emerging from a tradition that had rarely placed aesthetics at the center of research, Goffman's intense analysis of the minutia of social activity brought him to a deep appreciation of the aesthetics of face-to-face interaction – the artistry of the adroit bluff, the creativity of the skillful con. Emerging from a tradition that had insufficiently analyzed the linguistic and kinesic mechanisms by which expressive effects are achieved, performance scholars arrived at a detailed formal analysis of the techniques of folklore events – the apparatuses of keying and framing and the devices of reflexive language. Here, the sociologist of means/ends behavior becomes the consummate aesthete, while the scholars of expressivity become sociologists of linguistic and kinesic structure.

The interplay of these concerns is perhaps nowhere more evident than in Abraham's "Rhetorical Theory" article (1968) and in the second chapter of Bauman's *Verbal Art as Performance* (1977); these classic statements of performance theory illustrate how folklore performers manipulate the formal structures of verbal genres to achieve rhetorical goals and how artistic power can be converted into social power. Informed by this tradition, I have been sensitized to the intimate relationship between the expressive and the instrumental. These issues emerge most keenly in chapters 5 and 6, where I examine the consequences of passeggiata performance for the economic and personal lives of the townsfolk and explore the role of aesthetics in the Sassano ideology of modernity.

Style and the Social Life of the Body

Parallel to the performance-based research on costume and gesture are a number of works by British cultural studies scholars that explore the notion of style[5] (Polhemus 1994; Willis 1975, 1977; Cashmore 1987; Hebdige 1988; Forgacs and Lumley 1996). For example, examining youth music subcultures Dick Hebdige's work (1988) shows how the music, clothing, dances, and lifestyle choices of the English mods, rockers, and punks operate as symbolic statements of their subcultural ideologies. Similarly, Paul Willis's research (1975) on motorbike culture illuminates the ways in which the biker's styles of dress, interest in highly rhythmic music, attitudes about road safety, and concern for mastery over their machines serve as symbolic expressions of masculinity and group identity. Like the scholars of the folklife movement (Yoder 1963; Glassie 1982; Pocius 1991), the British analysts of style develop rich interpretations of social life by casting their nets wide and exploring an extremely broad range of expressive acts. Another advantage of this work is the ways in which it reveals how subcultural style is informed by large-scale power relations. Building on this approach, I have tried to attend to the diverse means through which style may be expressed in Sasso and to situate style within the contexts of class and gender.

One difficulty with older cultural studies approaches is the tendency to focus more on groups or historical movements than on individual social actors and to treat expressive practices merely as a reaction to larger social forces. For example, while E. Ellis Cashmore's discussion of British youth subcultures (1987) recognizes that there may be artistry in the music of the metalheads or the sartorial displays of the new romantics, he ultimately interprets such expressive culture as an escapist retreat from unemployment and degrading social conditions. Similarly, Willis's *Learning to Labour* (1977) treats the creativity of the working class "lads" that he studies as a response to social tensions that, in the final analysis, does nothing more than reproduce larger social inequities. Subordinating the aesthetic to the political, such work gives short shrift to the importance of expressivity in social life. My criticism here is not meant to disengage expressive culture from larger social contexts or call for a return to "art for art's sake" but to suggest that this work insufficiently explores the relationship of the aesthetic and the instrumental in everyday life. Following folklore's traditional emphasis on artistic behavior, I hope to explore more richly this complex interplay. And while my study does not claim to show how on-the-ground expressive culture constitutes large-scale social or economic phenomena, I hope to depict Sassani as the creative agents of their public performances and show that expressive culture can play a key role in ideologies of social change.

Related issues emerge in the humanistic and social scientific scholarship on the body. In a seminal 1936 article, Marcel Mauss (1973 [1936]) suggests that the body should be a focus of social inquiry and shows how activities such as walking, swimming, and squatting are culturally specific. While in the 1930s and 1940s some of Franz Boas's students explored body-related issues such as childbirth and sexuality (for example, Mead 1935), Mauss's call for an anthropology of the body received little attention until the 1960s and 1970s.[6] Coming from a range of disciplines, the early nonverbal communication scholars (Hall 1966; Birdwhistle 1972; Argyle 1975, 1976; Eakins and Eakins 1978) showed that it was possible to study body language in a detailed and systematic way. However, their attention to the micro-details of gesture and movement often failed to take into account the shaping influence of large-scale social contexts, especially inequities of power associated with class or gender. Such research tended to focus on the mechanics of bodily communication rather than its uses and meanings. Applying a behavioristic perspective to the decoding of bodily messages, these studies became mired in a concern for improving the methods for recording nonverbal interaction. These scholars operated under the assumption that human kinesics were fixed and stable and could be analyzed in a positivistic fashion.

Today, students of the body build upon the work of their predecessors but bring different concerns, orientations, and methods to the subject. Not only do contemporary scholars connect bodily practices to larger social contexts, they also treat the analysis of bodily communication as an interpretive process. In a special issue of *The Journal of American of Folklore* devoted to this topic (1994), Katharine Young maintains that, while bodily practices are informed by culture, they are also actively achieved. "The body is not simply inscribed by discourse," she explains, "it takes up discourse" (Young 1994, 3). Further, Deborah Kapchan's work on Moroccan dancers (1994) shows how the body can serve as a vehicle for complex ideological statements and how it is informed by local ideas about gender and religion. Her rich interpretations illustrate that, in Morocco, posture and gesture are perceived as manifestations of states of mind and are seen to possess a moral status (90). Such work cogently reveals how the bodies of dancing women in this culture seem "linguistically and corporeally loose, unbound, and transgressive" (88), and thus represent a locus of shamelessness and female power in North African culture.

Feminist scholars have also shown how the body is actively gendered by the process of socialization. There is tacit understanding in such work that cultural forces make men's and women's bodily engagement with the world markedly different. In her article "Throwing like a Girl," Iris Young (1990) traces out modalities of feminine comportment and illustrates how female motility is hampered by the sexism of contemporary Western culture. Young argues that the female person in patriarchy lives a "tension between transcendence and immanence, between subjectivity and being a mere object" (144) and shows that "as lived bodies, [women] are not open and unambiguous transcendences that move out to master a world that belongs to us, a world constituted by our own intentions and projections" (153). In a similar fashion, my analysis of the passeggiata will not only examine how women orient themselves through space but will also illustrate how comportment and gait combine with clothing and other elements of fashion in the highly gendered terrain of the piazza.

In Italy there is a long history of discourse about the body, and the writings of Renaissance thinkers inform the larger Italian culture in which Sasso is bathed. Interestingly these views articulate in surprising ways with contemporary scholarship on the body. Baldassare Castiglione's *Book of the Courtier* (1976 [1528]), for example, was both a prescriptive treatise on manners and bodily comportment and a detailed guide to the meanings of posture, gesture, and facial expression. Books of etiquette such as this insisted on upward training of the body. Here, straight bearing was metonymically associated with strength, poise, and virtue, and according to social historian George Vigarello (1989) the period's enthusiasm for proportion provided the justification for new requirements concerning physical bearing. As I suggest below such prescriptive notions have strong affinities with the present-day Sassano ideas of disinvoltura and *bella figura*. While contemporary research on the body has, of course, no prescriptive or universalistic thrust, folklorists like Katharine Young and Deborah Kapchan echo Castiglione's belief in the centrality of the body in social life and the moral significance of deportment, demeanor, and style.

While etiquette writers such as Castiglione saw themselves as instructors, Renaissance scholars like Giambattista Della Porta and Johann Lavatar saw themselves as scientist of the body (Magli 1989). Like Castiglione, however, their new science of "physiongnomics" expressed a constant concern with the correspondence between the inner and outer dimensions of the human form. Such scholars believed that the passions of the soul could be known from the particular shape of the body, and Della Porta and Lavatar sought to develop a science for interpreting the secret behind the human countenance (Magli 1989). Such ideas are consonant with a set of interpretive practices in contemporary Sasso which I call "bodily divination." Here, the towns-folk seek to gain insights into the inner, moral character of others by inspecting their passeggiata performances. In chapter 5, I will examine the complex set of aesthetic principles that inform bodily comport-ment in Sasso and the interpretative practices that people bring to the expressive acts of the promenade.

MEDITERRANEAN STUDIES, REFLEXIVE ETHNOGRAPHY, AND MODERNITY

The problems of modernity and expressive culture are not unique to Sasso, and two traditions of scholarship on this geographical area have been important to my study. While Mediterranean ethnography has supplied me with key models for interpreting the performance of gender in a changing social world, research on Italy has shed light upon the culturally specific dynamics of modernity and region.

Scholars of the Mediterranean such as Michael Herzfeld (1980, 1985, 1991), Jane Cowan (1990), and Jill Dubisch (1986) have devel-oped a theoretical groundwork for understanding the performance of gender and have shaped my thinking about Italian culture. For example, Herzfeld's *The Poetics of Manhood* (1985), an analysis of gender roles in a Greek village, maintains that past scholars have reinforced gender stereotypes by equating performance with the aggressive, male-dominated spheres of expressive culture and ignor-ing the more muted, female-oriented domains. He notes that the "difficulty [the scholar faces is not in] articulating a poetics of Greek women, but rather, [the belief] that poeticity lies only in the bombastic and verbal" (68). As Herzfeld and others have pointed out (Ardener 1975; Radner 1987), the "female discourse that shy away from ver-bality must be considered" (Herzfeld 1991, 67).[7] Jane Cowan's work on the Greek village of Soho does just that. In *Dance and the Body Politic in Northern Greece* (1990), Cowan shows how the ethnography of everyday sociability in weddings, coffeehouses, and social gather-ings can reveal insights into gender. In conceiving of dance as an event around which various social practices take place, Cowan widens our analytical lens and focuses our attention on women's experiences. Her work not only shows how mundane practices are organized in gender-specific ways but also demonstrates how a vari-ety of expressive behaviors (such as walking and posing) can be used to comment upon changing gender relations. According to Cowan, a young man's swagger is a visual and kinetic exemplar of Sohonian concepts of male assertiveness. Cowan views dance as an arena for performing, debating, and questioning notions of femaleness and maleness in Greek society. Following Cowan, my research uses bodily display to explore the diverse and varied ways that Sassani enact gender. As my study shows, gender is not merely an assigned label but something that is sensorially achieved, a dimension of identity that is produced, reproduced, and transformed in a changing world.

If Herzfeld (1990) and Cowan (1990) have emphasized the creative production of gender roles, a different group of contemporary scholars (Silverman 1975; Magliocco 1993; Romanucci-Ross 1991; Dubisch 1986) have shown how other elements of culture are negotiated and achieved in everyday life. Such work is in sharp contrast to past scholarship that depicted the Italian village as an isolated bastion of premodern cultural survivals (Pitrè 1913; Banfield 1958; Peristiany 1966). This approach can be traced back to the nineteenth-century Italian folklorist Giuseppe Pitrè, whose work depicted Sicilians as exotic Africans – a humble, nameless, forgotten "popolani" (little people) "who marched toward their evolutionary realization as Europeans" (Triolo 1993, 307). Pitrè represented both mafia and omertà (honor, respect) as rustic survivals of more heroic times. While his massive *Biblioteca delle tradizioni popolari siciliane* (*Compendium of Sicilian Folk Traditions*) is still considered an invaluable resource for Italian ethnographers, his romantic view of the Sicilian folk as primitive, premodern other clearly reflects the evolutionary biases of his day.

In the late 1950s and the 1960s, scholars from the "honor and shame school" of Mediterranean anthropology believed that the concepts of male honor and female shame were the basic organizing principles of culture in the region. Reducing the complexity of social experience to a small number of values and motivations, this perspective fostered a highly fatalistic and one-dimensional vision of Mediterranean culture. Echoing nineteenth-century models of social change that envision human society as evolving from premodern brutality to modern civility, Edward Banfield (1958), for example, represented the rural South of the 1950s as a backward and unevolved survival of an earlier time. Banfield's thesis of "amoral familism" (the idea that Sicilian culture is defined by clannishness and self-interest) sought to describe what he believed to be the dysfunctional aspects of peasant life in Sicily. Such an approach, Rosemary Coombe argues, reflected an "inability, or lack of desire, to explore cultural creativity, conflict, and resistance" (Coombe 1990, 221). Envisioning Sicilians as locked in the premodern past, this work ignored the fact that "culture [is] constantly reproduced, modified, and transformed by social agents"

(234). Herzfeld's concept of "disemia" highlights a similar point by drawing scholarly attention to the intricate contradictions that play out between abstract systems of thought and everyday social practices, such as the tensions that often exist between official and folk discourses and what Herzfeld describes as the dialectal relationship between "formalism" and "experience" in anthropological research (Herzfeld 1987, 135). Applying Herzfeld's ideas to the Honor and Shame school, I suggest that Mediterranean ethnographers of the past have often ignored the disemia that exists in their field sites and have focused on reified categories rather than lived social processes. According to Herzfeld, "what we must resist is the temptation to credit [binary codes] with coercive power over actors; for it is actors who use them" (Herzfeld 1987, 113). More recent research on urban Italy, however, has moved away from the reductionistic interpretations of Mediterranean society and contributed to a more variegated understanding of the region (Saunders 1983). The ethnographies of Sydel Silverman (1975), Alessandro Falassi (1980), Lola Romanucci-Ross (1991), and Sabina Magliocco (1993) have also shown how situated actors negotiate the broader forces of culture, politics, and public display in daily life.

If today's Mediterraneanists overcame the vestiges of evolutionary social theory in ethnography by attending to the dynamic quality of their field sites and refusing to see those sites as survivals of the premodern past, I hope to forward the contemporary project by drawing on ideas from the multiple modernities literature and critiquing the vision of modernity, rather than premodernity, offered in older developmental models. Exploring the passeggiata and other local forms of expressive culture, I seek to register the presence of modernity in Sasso. More importantly, though, I hope to highlight the culturally specific quality of that modernity, sensitizing researchers to the uniquely local perspectives on social change and problematizing notions of what a modern society can be.

Shortly after I arrived in Sasso, I took a walk in *I Crocetti* (The Crossroads area of Sasso) to search for the house in which my grandparents had lived. As I strolled along, an old woman in black attire perched on the tiny wicker chair in front of her house asked me, "*A chi appartieni?*" (Who do you belong to?). All too familiar with the importance of using clan names to identify lineage I replied, "*Sono la figlia di Nannine Fangiarilli*" (I am the daughter of Nannine Fangiarilli). After carefully looking me over she said, "*Ah sí adesso so chi sei, conosco la gente tua*" (Ah yes, I know who you are; I know your people). Pointing to a spot further up the street, she said, "*Lì sopra è dove abitavano tuo nonno e tua nonna e dove è cresciuta Nannine; cosi la chiamavamo"* (Up there, that's where your grandfather and grandmother lived, and where your mother, Nannine, was raised).

In many ways, my fieldwork in Sasso was an exploration of my own cultural past. Here, the other that I studied was indeed a partial self, and my ethnography of the town allowed me to reflect upon my own bicultural identity and my status as what Kirin Narayan (1992) has called a "halfie" – an ethnographer, often an immigrant or an ethnic, who is partially identified with the group being studied (see also Abu-Lughod 1991). At times during my fieldwork, Sassani saw me as one of their own, an insider with filial and cultural ties to the village. At other moments, however, I was the inquisitive outsider from abroad, and in many ways this betwixt-and-between situation felt quite familiar to me. In North America I grew up during the rising tide of Quebec nationalism and the heyday of Pierre Elliott Trudeau's campaigns for multiculturalism. Because of the identity politics of Canada, I was seldom seen as a full member of that society. First and foremost I was viewed as a hyphenated ethnic, the offspring of Italian immigrants. In the province of Quebec, the Minister of Cultural Communities and Immigration regularly came up with labels for distinguishing *Québécois de vieille souche* (Quebecker of old stock) from the newly transplanted. In this political climate I was alternately viewed as *une néo-Québécoise* (new Quebecker) or *une allophone* (an ethnic whose first language is neither French nor English) – even though I was born in Montreal and my parents spoke French. By no means was I considered *une Québécoise pure laine* (literally, a Quebecker of pure [virgin] wool), a term in nationalist discourse that was colloquially used to refer to those who could trace their ancestry to the often idealized rural Quebec of the eighteenth or nineteenth centuries. Paradoxically, it was in Italy that my Canadian nationality was most frequently recognized. There I was *la Canadese* (the Canadian) or *l'Americana* (the American) – a catch-all word which referred to anyone from overseas.

In both Sasso and Montreal, the various representations of national and ethnic identity that I experienced were bound up with discourses of modernity. In Quebec, rural Italy could be represented as either a premodern idyll or a land so hopeless and backward that hundreds of thousands were forced to flee. In Sasso, during both the family visits of my childhood and my adult fieldwork, Canada was alternatively depicted as a site of modern progress and wealth or a place where nouveau riches outmigrants lost their traditional Old World civility. While my "halfie" status did occasionally produce difficulties for me in the field, it also provided access to unique opportunities.

Drawing upon my background, I have, in both my fieldwork and my writing, turned to reflexive and autoethnographic techniques from contemporary scholarship to gain new insights into Sassano culture and the problem of modernity.

Beginning as early as the 1930s and picking up steam in the 1970s and 1980s, scholars from a range of discipline and orientations began to develop critiques of positivist approaches to ethnography. One strain of this tradition is centered on the notion of autoethnography, a term used most frequently in communication studies, education, and anthropology. A common feature among all the scholars who use this term is a desire to reveal the complex and subtle ways in which the researcher encounters and responds to others in ethnographic field-work. As a genre, autoethnography encompasses everything from first-person accounts to confessional autobiographies and literary tales (Ellis and Bochner 2000). Contrary to positivistic ethnography, it allows scholars to explore the complicated feelings that arise in the various stages of fieldwork and understand their emotional responses as at least a potential source of social insight. Beyond a common emphasis on the ethnographer's personal experience, the work of autoethnography can be highly diverse. For example, communication scholars Carolyn Ellis and Arthur Bochner view autoethnography as "an autobiographical genre of writing and research that displays multiple layers of consciousness, connecting the personal to the cultural" (Ellis and Bochner 2000, 739). Though anthropologist Deborah E. Reed-Danahay maintains an important difference between ethnography on the one hand and autobiography on the other hand, she too asserts that autoethnography is ostensibly a text that blends ethnography and autobiography (Reed-Danahay 1997). Some believe that the key characteristic of autoethnography is that here the scholar does not adopt the "objective outsider" convention of writing common to traditional ethnography (Reed-Danahay 1997, 6). Others simply define autoethnography (or autoanthropology) as "anthropology carried out in the social context which produced it" (Strathern 1987, 17).

Another anti-positivistic tradition in ethnographic research can be found clustered around the terms reflexive or experimental ethnography, and much of this work has its roots in the now famous "crises of representation" that anthropology began to face in the 1980s.[8] In their often cited work *Writing Culture* (1986), James Clifford and George Marcus challenged the basis of anthropological inquiry by arguing that ethnography constitutes a kind of literature. By laying bare the conventional tropes and literary devices that scholars use in ethnographic writing, Clifford and Marcus not only exposed the underlying politics of textual production, they have also problematized the field's more naive claims about its quest for objective and politically neutral truth. Their work has been instrumental in helping to recognize the contingent and partial nature of knowledge and in inspiring a generation of scholars to experiment with different voices and rhetorical styles. Of course Marcus and Clifford were not without predecessors. Ruth Behar and Deborah Gordon have criticized Clifford and Marcus for ignoring women's contributions to reflexive ethnography (Behar and Gordon 1995, 431), and their 1995 *Women's Writing Culture* highlighted both the path-breaking work of early feminist ethnographers and the more recent feminist developments in this area. Both within and beyond explicitly feminist scholarship, work in the reflexive tradition has sensitized scholars to the need for making ethnography more inclusive, participatory, collaborative, and democratic.

Though scholars of folklore's historic geographic method and certain thinkers in the Freudian tradition (for example, Ernest Jones 1965) saw their work as objective scientific descriptions, perhaps the majority in the field of folklore have taken a more interpretative approach to social research. If anthropology historically attended to cultural others, folklore's traditional study object (the peasantry of Western Europe) was closer to home. Though social class separated the nineteenth-century folklore collectors from their "informants," both parties often shared a common ethnic or national identity; indeed, the folklorists' "halfie" status (here, a shared national identity and an opposing class membership) was part and parcel of their larger nationalistic research program. By today's standards, some of this work may seem to be romanticizing and elitist. Nevertheless, the relationship between fieldworker and research participant has always been at the heart of folklore studies, and many contemporary ethnographers with critical programs (Farrer 1975; Jordan and Kalcick 1985; Goodwin 1989; Limon 1994) or an empathetic desire to understand their research participants on existential or human terms (Dégh 1969; Glassie 1982; Stahl 1989; Ives 1999) have used reflexive techniques in their work.[9] In *People Studying People* (1980), their classic book on field methods, Robert Georges and Micheal Owen Jones emphasized that the primary reality of ethnographic research is the social interaction between fieldworker and research participant. While there may be an objective quality to the data collected by these ethnographic methods, that data must be abstracted from its primary base in social interaction, and to be truly scientific, Georges and Jones argue, ethnographers have a responsibility to report on those interactions and the chain of biographical experiences that led them to the field in the first place. This kind of approach is evident in research found in many of folklore's areas of specialization. In the field of personal experience narrative, for example, Sandra Dolby draws upon the rich repertoire of narratives from her mother and members of her community to address issues of gender, class, and small-town life in the Midwest. In ethnomusicology, scholars such as Ruth Stone and Verlon L. Stone (1981) have used feedback interviews to garner native perspectives, draw their research participants into the fieldwork process, and make their inquiry more collaborative. Perhaps most importantly, feminist folklorists have highlighted how their own evolving feminist consciousness has shaped their choice of study objects and styles of collection, interpretation, and analysis (Farrer 1975; Radner and Lanser 1987; Jordon and Kalcik 1985; Boreland 1991; Lawless 1992; Sawin 2002).

Various threads from these diverse movements in ethnography have informed my approach to research. I follow Georges and Jones, for example, inasmuch as I have tried to show how my personal history led me to my research questions. Using experiences from own life to illuminate situations in the field – particularly experiences relevant to my halfie status – I draw on techniques of the autoethnography movement, and, like Ruth Behar, I use narratives from my own extended family to illustrate a larger historical process. I have found the feedback interview techniques of ethnomusicology to be particularly helpful in gaining richer, more polyphonic interpretations of visual performances, and the essays of *Writing Culture* certainly sensitized me to the politics of representation – specifically, the representations of regional identities in Italy.

While I believe that it is important to acknowledge the impact of the ethnographer upon the interview or participant/observation process, and, while I seek to understand how my own experiences have shaped the questions I ask and the answers I discover, I have been careful to avoid the overly self-involved stance that reflexive ethnographers have occasionally been accused of taking. Throughout, my goal has been to better understand Sasso and Sassani, and my reflections on my past, my family, and my own experiences in the field have been in the service of this goal. Finally, I must emphasize that humanistic ethnography is not opposed to addressing larger theoretical issues. While fieldworkers may dehumanize their research participants by treating them as mere examples of universal social processes, and while ethnography has often been implicated in oppressive colonialist projects, the goal of giving voice to subordinated perspectives need not cause us to abandon our search for social insight. In fact in my experience, Sassani were eager to hear my impression of life in their town, and they were not shy in expressing their views of North America or the nature of social life in general.

Indeed the particular leads to the general, and, by moving between Canada and Italy, the personal and the ethnographic, I hope to explore the various and complex visions of identity in Sassano culture. The central theme of these diverse visions is modernity. A site of urbanity and modern development or a rural village corrupted by consumerism; a place of burgeoning feminist consciousness or a town loosing its grip on traditional ways; the Southern tip of the Northern industrial zone or the Northern edge of the traditional South – Sasso is a place where identity is bound up with the problem of social change. The next chapter deepens our exploration of these issues by examining representations of local identity and modernity in a variety of discourses and spheres of social interaction.

3

Light Industry and Accordions: Representations of Contemporary Sassano Identity

Like the great social thinkers of the nineteenth century, Sassani are marked by a complex, ambivalent reaction to modernity, and the goal of this chapter is to explore how these reactions play themselves out in local discourse. Exploring both insider and outsider perspectives on the town, the first part of the chapter examines representations of Sasso from national and regional tourist literatures, local postcards, and a national television show. Focusing on local perspectives, the second part of the chapter uses interviews with the townsfolk, participant observation from everyday life, and an analysis of the local community games, *Giochi Senza Frontiere*, to shed light on Sassano ideas about modernity. This panoramic snapshot of contemporary life in Sasso will help us to understand better the larger social and ideological contexts in which the passeggiata is situated.

In the last twenty years, Sasso has seen strong economic growth due to a combination of tax incentives, cheap labor, and the industry connections of local officials. Its economic expansion has contributed to a higher standard of living and greater opportunities for the residents of Sasso and the surrounding villages. However, while many Sassani are grateful for their improved living conditions, they feel apprehensive about the future and the radical changes their community has undergone. The tangentopoli crises in Italy contributed to an even greater climate of uncertainty among the Italian electorate. The local corruption scandals in Sasso further exacerbated the townsfolk's increasing lack of faith in government. It is within this wider context of rapid social change and political turmoil that we must understand Sassani's ambivalence toward modernity.

POSTCARDS

Though I didn't think much about them in my childhood, postcards formed my earliest images of Italy. Throughout my youth my relatives spent summers visiting family in Sasso and regularly sent us souvenir postcards from the Old Country. My mother would typically display these commemorative photos in the glass front of our kitchen credenza, and as a child I remember wondering about the strange and unknown land from which my parents came. By their choice, my Italian-Canadian relatives usually embraced pastoral visions of village life in Italy. The postcards they sent us almost always depicted rural scenes of the landscape or breathtaking vistas of the Abruzzo's majestic mountains. In these representations, Italy is a premodern idyll, and, by implication, Canada is the land of modernity and social progress. While this vision is consonant with the representations of the Abruzzo produced by Italy's national tourist bureau, it is quite at odds with regional and local perspectives. This conflict of interpretations is part of a larger discourse about modernization, civility, and identity in Europe and the New World which I will return to throughout this study.

While I did not originally set out to study Sasso's postcards when I began my fieldwork, I soon realized that these images were a part of this discourse, and this became especially clear when I considered them in the light of their primary audiences. Described in the previous chapters, the history of migration and remigration in Italy is a reality of which every Sassano is keenly aware, and no local business person could produce postcards in Sasso without knowing that their main customers are outmigrants returning from abroad to vacation in their home town or members of the community dropping a wistful message to their relatives overseas. In this context, the postcards are a means by which local identity is represented and interpreted to far-flung audiences. For the new world relatives of vacationing outmigrants, the Sasso postcard that appears in their mailbox offers an image of the village life that they or their parents left behind. For local residents writing to their families abroad, the postcards are a representation of what the town has become. I clearly recall being fascinated as a child by the magazine photograph of Santa Cabrini, who peered at me from the kitchen table holding a heart of thorns or the Italian religious magazines *La Voce di Padre Pio* (The Voice of Padre Pio), which sat next to the phone. The postcards in my parent's home were part of my mental furniture, an element of domestic decoration of which I rarely took special note. I only realized how much the cards informed my vision of Sasso when, looking through magazines in the downtown tabaccheria (newspaper and cigarette shop that also sells stationary) one day early on in my fieldwork, I discovered a series of postcards I had never seen before. The newer images clashed with those from my childhood, and it was the strange reaction I had toward these more recent representation that lead me to appreciate the wider significance of this visual genre.

This section will examine the national and local views of Sassano society through a rhetoric of the landscape. In the popular imagination, the modest agrarian folk from the mountainous region of the Abruzzo all live in isolated hilltop communities unencumbered by the forces of civilization. Both drawing upon and reinforcing these ideas, the national tourist literature represents the region as a bastion of rural antiquity and premodern isolation.[1] For example, on the front page of an official brochure from *Il museo delle genti d'Abruzzo* (Museum of the People of the Abruzzo) there is a passage by the noted writer Ignazio Silone that romantically evokes the landscape of the region and the important role of nature in the Abruzzese experience. Waxing poetic, Silone says:

The destiny of the men of the region which in the last eight centuries has been called the Abruzzo was principally decided by the mountains ... The Abruzzesi have remained in isolated communities that share a singular destiny and are characterized by a tenacious loyalty to economic and social forces beyond their control. This would be inexplicable if one didn't account for the constant fact of their existence, the most primitive and stable of elements: nature.

A more recent publication by the government tourist organization Comunità Montana (literally, Mountain Organization; a government tourist office) similarly praises the region's natural wildlife and rural antiquity but adds an ecological twist. On the front cover of the pamphlet, there is a photo of a wooded area; superimposed over this photo is a drawing of a green-colored heart, and underneath the entire image is a caption that reads *Un cuore verde da scoprire!* (A Green Heartland to Discover!). The introduction shows a photograph of three boys hiking into the woods while the text below says, "*Alla scoperta di immagini, suoni, colori, sapori della nostra terra*" (Upon the discovery of images, sounds, colors, and tastes of our land). On the opposite side of the page the visual imagery is enhanced by an evocative textual description of the region's local delicacies and rich folk traditions. The passage reads:

La contenuta bellezza dei paesaggi, il silenzio dei borghi, la particolare atmosfera rievocano la vita semplice di un tempo e propiziano il culto delle tradizioni fatto di prelibatezze gastronomiche, semplici e genuine, di poesia folkloristica, purezza arti-gianale. Attraversando la nostra Comunità si riscopre anche un modo nuovo di mettersi in contatto con la natura.

By traveling in our area, we rediscover a new way of getting into contact with nature. The silence and beauty of the countryside and the invigorating fresh air evokes the simple life of a traditional time with its simple and genuinely delicious cuisine, folk poetry, and artisinal purity. By walking through our community we rediscover a new way of reconnecting with nature.

In these scenes, the tourist can take a trip into the unspoiled past and rediscover the wonders of rural simplicity. Here, the city dweller can experience the joys of outdoor living and the delightful pleasures of traditional folk cuisine. This temporary excursion back to the land allows people to escape the pressures of modern life and experience moments of reflection and introspection. In this tourist paradise, human beings are replenished and made whole again.

However, while the national representations of the region celebrate nature, the locally produced postcards of Sasso highlight their economic development. The governmental leaders of Sasso clearly have a vested interest in touting their achievements to outsiders – not only to gain political capital, but also to attract prospective investors. By showcasing its modern facilities and expanding urban landscape, Sassano leaders point to a promising social base for future development. To appeal to corporations and the legislative support for wildlife preservation and tourism, Sasso's postcards depict the town as the best of both worlds – a home to both the modern conveniences of a big city and the idyllic beauty of a rural life.

In the past, the typical Sassano postcard usually featured the downtown church and piazza. One of the bestsellers from the late 1960s is cast against a cheerful summer sky and shows a frontal view of the statue of the Madonna serenely overlooking the town square (figure 20). The souvenir image of this period almost always had as its focal point Sasso's main thoroughfare, Corso Vittorio Emanuele, and scenes of its beautifully manicured gardens, located in the central square.

In today's postcards, Sasso presents a harmonious synthesis of continuity and change. By juxtaposing its traditional places of worship against the symbols of modernity, old and new are wedded to reflect the transformations that have occurred in the community. One two-tiered, vertical postcard illustrates these themes with clarity. While the first frame of the postcard has the Santa Lucia chapel peering through a shady pine forest, the bottom frame displays a panoramic photograph of Sasso's recently built polisportivo (recreational center) nestled against delicately sloping hills and an immense blue sky

Figure 20   Postcard of the piazza in Sasso; note the statue of the Madonna
overlooking the street (Ed. Gaspari-Riv.Tab.)

(figure 21). With its conference facilities, bar, tennis courts, and sport-
ing field, the polisportivo is a source of pride in the town. A similarly
inspired photomontage provides an illustration of the freshly landscaped, historic church of Maria Addolarata next to an image of
Sasso's modern hospital (figure 22). In these postcards both past and
present, sacred and profane coexist, alongside one another.[2]

     While these images of Sasso are extremely common in the local
tabaccheria, there is one tourist postcard which defies these conven-
tions by excluding any recognition of the town's rural past. The
postcard displays a long view of a suburban housing development in
the town and Sasso's Olympic-sized public swimming pool (figure 23).
Here, the government-sponsored low-income housing stands next to
the Sasso's latest monument to social progress. As with other postcards of this genre, however, the Abruzzese mountains, trees, and
immense blue sky are always present and are used to frame even the
most modern symbols of scientific advancements.

     The postcard with the Maria Addolarata church is another interesting
anomaly (figure 22). In the past, Sassano postcards always featured
the San Michele church, a modern, octagonally shaped structure built
in the 1960s; however, today's growing affluence has helped spawn
an interest in the historic buildings situated in the older quarters of
town. Even though the Maria Addolarata church has suffered damage
from neglect over the years, there has been a movement afoot in Sasso

Figure 21   Postcard of the Santa Lucia
Chapel and the polisportivo (sports center)
(Ed. Gaspari-Riv.Tab.)

Figure 22   Postcard of the Maria Addolorata Church and Sasso's modern hospital
(Ed. Gasparia-Riv.Tab.Cart)

Figure 23   Postcard of suburban housing development
and Olympic-sized swimming pool (Ed. Gasparia-Riv.Tab.
n. 1)

to restore it to its original state. In Sasso, the San Michele church has
increasingly fallen out of favor with young professionals, who prefer
to have their weddings held in the historic Maria Addolarata. But this
admiration for *la parte vecchia* (the old part of town) is not widely
shared by all Sassani. Most of the older Sassani do not understand
the fascination with the old and prefer the conveniences of modern
housing. In the last five years, however, some families from Naples
have bought and repaired a few of the older, damaged houses from
the area and transformed them into summer cottages.[3]

When I first arrived in Sasso the people with whom I spoke openly
venerated their monuments to social progress. Person after person
proudly pointed to the newly built hospital and Olympic-sized

swimming pool and boasted of the radical changes the community had undergone in the last few decades. As the months wore on, however, I began to hear another refrain. As I explain below, most of the people who live in Sasso welcomed their higher standard of living; however, many Sassani mourned the loss of simpler times and deplored what they believed to be the evils of consumption.

Despite Sassano misgivings about modernity, they see themselves as cosmopolitan urbanites who share close ties with their agricultural roots. They are, on the one hand, sophisticates who abhor outdoor camping; on the other hand, they enjoy their holiday scampagnate (picnics) in the country massaria (farm houses), where they feast on ventricina (spicy sausage made with pork, red pepper, and fennel) barbecued capretto (lamb), wine, and Abruzzese grappa (a local liquor). These citified folk take pride in their community's progress but also embrace their peasant past. Self-avowed moderns, they continue to harness the power of the land by practicing weekend farming and making wine from the locally harvested grapes. Many Sassani make or buy domestically produced olive oil from Sasso's orchards. They occasionally take jaunts with family and friends into the woods to look for asparagus, which is used for making frittate (Italian-style omelettes), or moss, which is used for covering nativity scenes at Christmas. Even the Sassani's favorite pastime, the passeggiata, integrates a background period in the rural park before people get underway with the ritual display of style and good manners.

The civic boosterism that runs rampant in Sassano postcards reflects the vision of the local political elites. While Sasso is far from being an Edenic paradise, in some ways it does indeed have the best of both the modern and the traditional worlds. By the same token, it also possesses the failings of both worlds; as I shall explain below, locals often complained about raccomandazioni, youth unemployment, isolation, and tedium. Ultimately, what we see in Sasso are the ways in which the traditional and the modern overlap in the present moment – with both positive and negative consequences for the people who live there. The postcards also illustrate the glaring incongruity between local and national representations of contemporary life in the Abruzzo. The tension between local and national views are nowhere more evident than in the national media's representation of Sasso during the tangentopoli scandal.

SASSO ON NATIONAL TELEVISION: GIULIANO FERRARA'S *L'ISTRUTTORIA*

In the winter of 1992, the nationally syndicated television program *L'Istruttoria* (court hearing) devoted two hours to the political scandals of the Abruzzo and the small community of Sasso. An example of what Italians call *televisione spazzatura* (literally, filth television; tabloid journalism), *L'Istruttoria* uses highly theatrical techniques to explore the social and political issues of contemporary society. On this episode, the guest roster included a live studio audience in Rome, a large group of people from Sasso (including Sasso's mayor, Guido Lantenari, and most of the town's political establishment), and Fulvio Neve, a representative from the regional branch of the opposition party Rifondazione Comunista. Both Neve and the Sassano politicos could be seen by the studio audience in Rome; the Sassano politicians spoke from Sasso's recreational center, while the leader of Rifondazione Comunista was located in his political stronghold of Teramo. The studio audience in Rome was comprised of members of the general public and career politicians from various parties. Also present in Rome was Renato Piove, a Sassano resident and outspoken critic of the local government who almost unseated Lantenari in the previous election.

To understand the proceedings, a small amount of background is necessary. In 1992, a young engineer's complaints against the Abruzzo regional executive prompted the arrest of the entire provincial council. The ranking system that the council used to evaluate the merits of development projects was found to be corrupt, and a number of politicians were sent to prison. This event also brought to light the misappropriation of millions of dollars, which later prompted the *mani pulite* operation (literally, the clean hands operation; an investigation of political corruption among high ranking officials in the Italian parliament). According to journalist Sergio Turone, the nation's tangentopoli crises can be directly traced to the debacle that occurred in the Abruzzo council in 1992 (Turone 1993). During this period, many dissatisfied Abruzzesi who had historically voted for the conservative Democratic Christian Party, cast their vote for the right-wing New Alliance Party (the former neofascist Movimento Sociale Italiano, or MSI), which promised greater political accountability and fiscal restraint.

The local corruption scandals in Sasso also attracted a great deal of media attention. The Italian RAI 3 and French Antenne 2 television networks both did extensive investigative pieces on the political graft in Sasso and, in particular, on Lantenari, an influential elder statesman of the then ruling Christian Democratic Party. As we will see in our analysis of *L'Istruttoria*, Sasso was held up as an object lesson in tangentopoli and the festering moral decay of a failing bureaucratic system. Accusations of raccomandazioni and unfair hiring practices made the headlines. In the summer of 1993, twenty-seven people in

Sasso were served with subpoenas and held under house arrest. Many Sassani were elated by the arrests and took great pleasure in seeing local politicians receive their just deserts. At the time of the scandal, rumor had it that a bag of feces had been placed on the front steps of the home of a well-known health official; another rumor held that the same official had a scarecrow placed in his backyard – a sign commonly understood as a threat.

It was into such a context that this episode of *L'Istruttoria* was launched. A heavy set man with a highly theatrical manner, Giuliano Ferrara begins the program with his typical dramatic flare. In a *sotto voce*, conspiratorial tone, Ferrara turns to Fulvio Neve and asks him about the anti-mafia march that is scheduled for next week. In the dimly lit studio the cameras are rolling but Ferrara's theatrical style of presentation suggests the backstage behavior reserved for private parlor conversations. Then suddenly the larger-than-life host breaks the frame by shifting his attention to his audience. Handcuffed and smoking a cigar, Ferrara dramatically announces the show's topic of discussion – the accusations made against Abruzzesi politicians. From the outset the program is presented as an istruttoria, a preliminary hearing for determining future grounds for indictment. In the role of the hardboiled prosecutor, Ferrara slowly reveals bits of tantalizing information about the scene of the crime and the cast of characters.

During Ferrara's opening statement, two policemen in full regalia stand next to a traditionally clad pair of folk dancers and a folk musician with a *ddu botte* (a traditional Abruzzese accordion); all are nervously standing in the back waiting for their cues to perform. After a few moments of confusion, the accordion player softly begins a traditional Abruzzese folk song, while Ferrara continues with his introduction. It is clear that the performers are made uncomfortable by the belligerence of the host and the burlesque roles in which they have been cast.

Against the backdrop of the subdued music, Ferrara freely associates about the current political situation in the Abruzzo. Speaking in a series of fragmentary and disjointed remarks, Ferrara says, "*Abruzzo vocazione rurale, oltre manette e decenti storie, ci mancano solo le pecore. Abruzzo è rimasto lo stesso, o è solo peggiorato?*" (Abruzzo rural vocation, beyond handcuffs and gossip, missing are only the sheep. The Abruzzo has it stayed the same, or has it only gotten worst?). With staccato, almost telegraphic delivery, he suggests that, "*L'Abruzzo si è fatto cattiva fama … vocazione Europea, classe dirigente, simulacri, giunta regionale dissolta, tutti in galera*" (Abruzzo has achieved a bad fame, European, dominant class, foil, regional executive dissolved, everybody in jail).

His statements are filled with innuendo and allusion and read like disconnected tabloid headlines. In his bombastic style, Ferrara uses the symbols of Abruzzese folk culture – the sheep and the *ddu botte* – to disparage the people who live in the region. In so doing, he raises questions about the Abruzzo's social progress and insinuates that these agrarian folk are a survival of Italy's premodern past, or may actually be regressing to an earlier stage of cultural evolution. At best, Ferrara wryly suggests, these uncivilized *contadini* (peasants) may still be tending to their sheep and living in a haze of feudal isolation. Throughout the broadcast, Ferrara depicts Sasso as a classic southern town and draws on stereotypes of the Mezzogiorno (literally, the midday region; the South) as a hotbed of crime and patronage.

With a disdainful tone of voice, Ferrara then introduces Sasso to the nation by referring to it as *"piccola, ma calda cittadina di Sasso"* (the small but steamy town of Sasso). The studio audience and the viewers watch as Sasso's marching band performs a festive piece of music in the town's polisportivo. Back in Rome the audience members are shown laughing at the inappropriate display of pomp and ceremony, especially given the program's theme – graft and corruption. Poking fun at the display of solidarity in Sasso, Ferrara sarcastically asks, "Are there any dissenters? All friends?" Next, Ferrara presents Renato Piove, Guido Lantenari, and Fulvio Neve.

Once the three main guests are introduced, Ferrara briefly summarizes the events that led to the incarceration of the Abruzzo's regional executive. He states, "Papers were seized, interrogations were underway." Lapsing into dramatic alliteration, Ferrara adds, *"Manette e mazzette"* (literally, handcuffs and blocks of bank notes; the phrase is best translated as "handcuffs and kickbacks"). Thunder and the sound of breaking glass announce a commercial break. The evening's subject is in place.

L'Istruttoria is no different from any other form of theater. In many ways, the show is less about the news than about the sense of drama that the host tries to generate. Ferrara uses props, sound effects, and live actors to stir up the emotions of his viewers. He even modulates his voice for effect and alternates between whispers and vitriolic exposition to the audience. His huge stature and belligerent manner lend the show a greater sense of melodrama. Irony and double entendres abound, and the atmosphere is one of bread and circuses.

In the next segment of *L'Istruttoria*, the conversation revolves around bribes, kickbacks, and the mismanagement of European Community development funds. Political representatives share their views and provide commentary. Officials from different parties make statements urging the Italian courts to follow proper legal procedure in their investigations. Both Communist and Democratic Christians express their displeasure at the swift actions that was taken against the Abruzzo's regional council and claim that those who were arrested were treated unfairly by the courts. Many thought the arrest premature and a threat to the constitutional rights of Italian citizens. Other issues were discussed briefly: constitutional immunity and the jurisdictional power of the attorney general.

At the time of these exchanges Ferrara disrespectfully refers to Sasso's mayor as "zio Guido" (uncle Guido). The mayor retorts by saying that he is an uncle only to his nephews and nieces. Ferrara routinely uses denigrating forms of address to speak to Lantenari. By borrowing well-known labels from the press such as the *imperatore dell'isola felice* (emperor of the isle of joy) and *padre padrone* (father/boss-exploiter) Ferrara designates Lantenari as an icon of Italian patronage.

One of the main points of contention among the speakers in the program was the European Community's system of ranking, which was used to determine which projects received public funding. The rules set by the European Community recommend the use of a graduatoria (ranking system) that attributes points based upon clearly defined parameters such as merit, need, and feasibility. Despite these guidelines, the Abruzzese council distributed funds according to older criteria that allowed officials greater discretionary power. To point out how money had been flagrantly mismanaged, one politician reads a list of absurd projects that were deemed worthy of support. She describes how public funds were approved for the installation of an artificial snow machine that could only be used if the nearby hotel was booked to nearly full capacity. In another example, the construction of a bowling alley was filed under the auspices of a private enterprise belonging to a member of the regional government. The list included the endorsement of facilities in which members had a financial interest and the construction of buildings which were unnecessary to the community.

In the two-hour broadcast there are also two short news segments. The first report deals with the case of the Abruzzo's regional council, while the second piece includes an interview with a health official who is being accused of wrongdoing. With his typical, melodramatic style, Ferrara frames the health-related case before it even gets under way, saying, "We will see the testimony of a man who is visibly scared and disillusioned with the corrupt government to which he belongs." A member of the audience defends the honesty of the accused and suggests that it was the corrupt system of politics that had compromised the official. Embroidering upon an earlier plot thread, Ferrara refers to the official as a political pentito (remorseful sinner), and in so doing conjures up Italy's famous mafia trials and its pentiti (literally, the contrite ones; the mafioso who turned state's evidence). Evoking classic stereotypes of the mafia-ridden South, Ferrara represents the Abruzzo as another underdeveloped province plagued by the "southern problem." The Christian image of pentimento is not only rhetorically powerful but especially resonant in a culture such as that of Italy, which has a long tradition of Catholicism.

During his performance, Ferrara is a Janus-faced figure, a trickster who likes to play word games and lull his audience into a false sense of security. He is the consummate polemicist, taking pleasure in his own verbal artistry and argumentative skills. Through words and images, Ferrara can muster the emotional intensity of his viewers and influence Italian public opinion. For Ferrara's purposes, television is a weapon and a tool of persuasion.

One of the most embarrassing moments in *L'Istruttoria* occurs when Sasso's mayor, in a fit of anger, stands up from his chair to intimidate verbally an opponent who is trying to speak his mind. This lack of decorum does not win the mayor any friends that night; he demonstrates no self-control and embarrasses his community on national television. These scenes elicits guffaws from the viewers at RAI 3 headquarters. In the same Rome studio only a few seconds later, Renato Piove nervously accuses Sasso's mayor of cronyism and proceeds to describe a long list of people who were on the unemployed roster and were never called for job interviews because of their Communist allegiance. Lantenari smiles and claims he cannot be held accountable for firing and hiring since he is not the *datore di lavoro* (employer).

The situation in Sasso escalates. A man with a grievance against the town's government approaches the microphone, and supporters of the mayor try to surround him and drown out his words. The female reporter at the polisportivo urges people to calm down and tries to bring order to the ruckus. Ferrara pleads with the audience to let the opponent speak, but there is too much confusion to understand what anybody is saying. In an attempt to refocus the discussion, Ferrara asks the members of the town council if they have anything to say, but all decline comment. After the chaos subsides, the mayor states that the disruption was caused by seven or eight provocateurs from the outside who were brought in by the Rifondazione Comunista. In the studio in Rome, people are laughing, and Ferrara sarcastically asks if the people at the meeting suffer from *sindrome da accerchiamento* (ambush syndrome).

Many Sassani felt ashamed by what had occurred on *L'Istruttoria*. Their local leaders misbehaved on national television and had given their town a bad name. *"Sasso ha fatto brutta figura quella sera"* (Sasso made a bad public face that evening), many people told me. In his public display of anger, Sasso's mayor looked like a temperamental mafioso who had lost control of his underlings. Given the scandal mongering antics for which Ferrara was known, one might wonder what possessed the citizens of Sasso to even participate in the show. It is clear from my exchanges with the Communist dissenter who spoke from the Rome headquarter that he relished the opportunity to criticize the shenanigans of the administration, and I believe that the local mayor, knowing full well that his opponent was going to try to discredit him before a national audience, felt that he had no choice but to rebut the accusations that he knew would be levied against him.

From the outset, Ferrara had predetermined the fate of Sasso in this "hearing" and resorted to regional stereotypes to interpret the political scandals of the Abruzzo. In his representation, centrally situated Sasso becomes a part of the underdeveloped South, and Sassani become classic Southerners – a simple rural popolino (little people) who depend on their tyrannical leaders for survival. Using a wide range of theatrical devices, he fosters great emotional intensity in his audience and enflames the hearts of his viewers. In this bombastic melodrama about the Italian state and the arrogant use of power, Ferrara ultimately assuages the fears of Romans by suggesting that crime and corruption exist at a safe distance from the modern centers of national power. Ultimately, Ferrara's discourse is an enlightenment discourse, equating the modern with progress and the premodern with corruption. Caught in the crossfire of these larger cultural tropes, Sasso becomes nothing more than an anachronism, an embarrassing survival of Italy's feudal past.

THE COURT OF PUBLIC OPINION

While Ferrara's discourse is a simple condemnation of the premodern, Sassani themselves expressed a complex ambivalence toward modernity. Though the town had benefited from national development initiatives and the political privilege of its leaders, the tangentopoli crisis left Sassani wondering about their children's future and the solvency of the Italian state. While they denounced the evils of consumption, Sassani also embraced the power of technology. Based on formal interviews and casual conversations, this section explores local representations of Sassano identity and reveals the rich mix of negative and positive feelings that the townsfolk have – about both modernity and themselves.

When I arrived in Sasso in March of 1993 the *mani pulite* operation had already begun to expose the corruption in the Italian state bureaucracy. The old system of patronage was under attack and high-ranking officials had already been tried and jailed. In Sasso, people were disenchanted with the local politics of the town and the criminal allegations made against their mayor. Sasso's much maligned leader, however, commanded a great deal of respect from some members of the community. As one person told me, "*Ha fatto assai per il paese e la regione; ha fatto costruire l'ospedale, le fabbriche, ha dato lavoro a tante persone. È vero che è stato sfacciato e cattivo molte volte e ha preferito certe famiglie, però non dobbiamo dimenticare che se non fosse per lui e il suo potere il paesino sarebbe rimasto un piccolo paesino senza niente da offrire alla gente.*" (It's true, he did a great deal for the town and the region; he had the hospital built, factories, gave work to many people. It's true that he was ruthless and he favored certain families, but we can't forget that if it wasn't for him the town would have stayed a small little village with nothing to offer.)

In everyday conversation, Sassani often expressed strong misgivings about their town's growing prosperity and the benefits of modernity. Some Sassani believed that they had wrongfully benefited from the work of corrupt politicians and envisioned a day when the guilty would have to pay for their greed. In a quasi-religious tone, an older seamstress I interviewed told me, "*La gente sarà punita per i suoi peccati*" (People will be punished for their sins). She maintained that, on this day of judgment, the people who participated in the politics of *raccomandazioni* would be held accountable for their actions. Most of all, those who suffered at the hands of the old regime would finally get their day in court and, in so doing, help to usher in a new era in local government.

Other Sassani spoke admiringly of the frugal ways of the past. Graziella, a sixty-five-year-old widow, told me, "*Dovremmo tornare ai vecchi tempi quando la vita era più semplice, però eravamo contenti*" (We should go back to the old days when life was simpler, but we were happy). She envisioned a time when the political corruption of the Italian state and the rampant consumerism of the population would lead to an economic collapse; in these post-apocalyptic times, the traditional home economy would be valued once again. The nostalgic longing for rural independence reveals a desire to escape the corruption and greed of contemporary Italian culture. This positive vision of self-reliance paints a rosy picture of the past and rarely acknowledges the hardship of *la miseria* (the depression immediately following the Second World War), during which half the population of Sasso emigrated abroad.

Despite the glorification of the past, Sassani also sang the praises of technology. In a place where women remember going to the well daily to draw water, the wonders of modern indoor plumbing cannot be underestimated. My mother's classic stories about her treks to the well with her conca (copper water bucket) are part of her repertoire of narratives about the Old Country; these stories, which I heard repeatedly throughout my childhood, were intended to remind me of the comforts of life in Canada. Francesca Puccini, who had lived in Philadelphia and came back to retire in Sasso, remembers the unsanitary and inefficient means of waste disposal from the old days. She said, *"La puzza, non ti dico, non era sana; e poi la cacca dei cavalli sul corso, che schifo."* (The stench was unbearable, I can't describe it. It was unhealthy. The shit from the horses – disgusting.) Many Sassano housewives who, as little girls, did the laundry in the local fountains, were especially grateful for appliances which freed them from the drudgery of hand-washing. In Sasso, people also had great reverence for the telephone and Italy's modern system of highways, which allowed for more efficient methods of travel. Today in Sasso almost all the offices around town have access to fax machines, and many of the local business people feel compelled to own a cell phone.

Sassani, however, do not all look favorably upon modern-day social advancements and the broader changes that have occurred in Italian society. As Emilia, a middle-aged housewife told me, *"Le ragazze vanno a spasso per la strada; si truccano e frequentano i ragazzi in giovane età"* (Young girls loiter around the streets; they wear makeup and date boys at a young age). On more than one occasion Sassani expressed their disdain for the young women who spent their time roaming around the piazza. They would tell me, *"Non combinano niente, imparano solo cose non buone. Perchè non rimagono a casa ad aiutare le loro madri?"* (They achieve nothing, they learn only bad things. Why don't they stay home to help their mothers?). Many of the older Sassani believed that modernity had only fostered idle consumption and made people complacent. In their opinion, social change not only undermined the values of hard work and sacrifice, it also threatened traditional notions of womanhood. I will discuss the modernization of gender roles in chapter 4.

By contrast, the performance of domestic diligence was highly admired by the older Sassani. In the early morning hours of the weekdays, a flurry of housewives routinely descends upon the piazza to run errands and do the day's shopping. Such ritual displays of busyness were intended for viewing and embodied the ideals of female enterprise and industriousness that some Sassani felt lacking in the younger generation of women. In Sasso, the ideal housewife seeks to have all her chores done by morning so she can devote the rest of the day to cooking an elaborate dinner for her family. These daily tasks, however, are also conditioned by Sassano store hours; local businesses close at 1:00 p.m. and only reopen later at 4:00 p.m. Government offices and banks provide even less flexibility for their clients, as they close their doors by 2:00 p.m.

The town's growing prosperity helped fan the flames of local rivalry and the longstanding antagonisms between villages. On more than one occasion, I heard people from the surrounding villages of Flavio and Roccaspina speak of Sassani with contempt and accuse them of being self-aggrandizing, ignorant petit bourgeois. At times, this deep dislike for Sasso manifested itself in extreme ways. At a local café one night, an acquaintance from Flavio told me that he preferred to take the older, less convenient route to Sasso because it fell under his town's jurisdiction. Even non-natives who have now made Sasso their home often describe the villagers as mean and ostentatious. In an interview with a nursing student who attends school in Sasso, Maria said to me, "*I Sassani sono cattivi, Giovanna; hanno un altro atteggiamento*" (Sassani are mean, Giovanna; they have another attitude).

The harshest criticisms of Sassani, however, often come from the residents themselves. In hushed murmurs, Sassani often displayed a deep antipathy toward their own paesani and those with whom they share kinship ties. While I was browsing through her store, one middle-aged woman confessed to me, "*Si sono fatti la testa grande*" (They [other Sassani] all have swollen heads). Others spoke of the closed-minded mentality that hides behind the self-congratulatory patina of cosmopolitanism that locals tout to outsiders. "*I Sassani non sono aperti, sono diffidenti, non ti puoi fidare*" (Sassani are not open, they're diffident, you can't trust them), said a Sasso businessman. I have also heard local shopkeepers malign their fussy Sassano clients for being fickle and presumptuous. "*Non sono mai soddisfatti, non sanno quello che vogliono e si lamentano sempre. E che arie, mamma mia!*" (They're never satisfied, they don't know what they want and they always complain. They have such hoity toity attitudes!)

The highly critical perception that Sassani have of one another may simply be a function of the tensions that develop in any small group. Here, the social ties that unite and divide the townsfolk contribute to the complex mixture of self-hatred and civic pride. With its rampant cronyism, it is almost unthinkable for a person in Sasso to secure even unskilled employment without *una raccomandazione* (a reference from a respected member of the community). The divisive politics and scarce job opportunities produce a climate of distrust and diffidence and have exacerbated feelings of powerlessness among the residents.

On a deeper level, however, I believe Sassani's contempt for their town reveals the displaced anger they have toward their local politicians. Further, the resentment they harbor toward other members of their community may actually obscure the feelings of guilt they have about their own complicity in the clientalistic politics of the town. When they speak harshly about Sasso, they may be projecting their own feelings of self-hatred onto other members of the village who perhaps feel equally compromised by a system they abhor.

The complex emotional bonds that divide Sassani also bring them together in their common dislike for the residents of the surrounding villages. This repertoire of traditional insults is an established part of Sassano folklore. Such names are believed to reveal the inherent personality flaws of the townsfolk in question, and the significance of these terms is an occasional topic of conversation in Sasso. For example, the people from Flavio are referred to as "pitzanti" (poor devils), while those from Roccaspina are called *"culo a pese"* (literally, those who drag their behinds). "Cafoni" (the ignorant hillfolk) is used to refer to Bevilaquans. Sassani themselves have earned the title of *"cocia cavutitti"* (dialect for "people with holes in their heads"). Admittedly few people openly advocate these village stereotypes, but even the less ardent proponents of this lore resort to name-calling to explain negative interactions with non-natives.

Despite the rivalries between villages and Sasso's internal antagonisms, Sassani are proud of the distinctive place their town occupies in the region. For the villages in the surrounding area, and for Sassani themselves, Sasso is an icon of modernity. It is a center of commerce and light industry and offers all the amenities of a big city. The town has a wide array of facilities including a hospital, recreational center, and business school. Many of the residents from the neighboring villages come to Sasso to do their banking and shopping.

In popular memory, Sasso has often been viewed as a cosmopolitan village with close affinities to the nearby coastal centers. Sassani affectionately refer to their town as *"la piccola Parigi dell'Abruzzo"* (the little Paris of the Abruzzo) and point to their attractive thoroughfare and well-known passeggiata as a sign of their civiltà. Many Sassani like to think of themselves as enlightened folks and tout their accomplishments to outsiders. When I was growing up in Montreal, my mother, a native of Sasso, would frequently brag about Sassani's innately superior character and their eagerness to embrace the precepts of modern life. She often reminded me that *"I Sassani sono sempre stati più aperti e civili della gente degli altri paesi"* (Sassani have always been more open-minded and civilized than those from the nearby villages).

In the disagreements between my parents, my mother would usually attribute my father's contrary views to his non-Sassano status; this would then prompt my father to insult my mother with disparaging remarks about her town. I was often amused by my parent's use of village labels to discredit one another in verbal disputes. This repartee struck me as melodramatic and absurd, but these words exercised great power over my parent's lives and taught me firsthand about the strength of village allegiances.

The ambivalent and emotional interpretations of Sassano identity and modernity spawned by the tangentopoli crisis take on added significance when placed in the context of the history of Abruzzese outmigration. For those who celebrated Sasso's economic and social advancement, the scandals call into question the legitimacy of the town's much touted prosperity. If the economic affluence of the 1970s and 1980s seemed to provide comfort to those townsfolk who chose not to emigrate to other countries, tangentopoli placed the wisdom of their choices in doubt and revived the worst images of Italian society – a place of economic stagnation, cronyism, and corruption. How can we hold our town up to our overseas relatives as an icon of modernity, many Sassani wondered, when our future is so uncertain? For those segments of the population who did not see themselves as benefiting from the post-1960s boom and perhaps regretted the decision to stay behind – communist supporters and other politically marginalized residents, families without powerful contacts, older working-class women who did not enjoy the possibilities offered by the broadened gender roles – the revelations of the *mani pulite* operation were a vindication of their criticism of the new Sassano modernity.

As we can see, the responses to larger social processes are never simple or neat: they are fraught with contradictions and tensions. The complex meanings Sassani bring to the social changes that they have experienced ultimately reveal a traditional apprehension and a suspicious stance toward modernity. For the residents of this small, hilltop village and the surrounding communities, Sasso is an exemplar of progress, and the ambivalent feelings Sassani have toward their home town reflect a larger ambivalence about social change. Content to enjoy the fruits of technology and economic prosperity, Sassani nevertheless fear the corrupting influence of consumption. Proud of their cosmopolitanism and resistant to the jibes of nearby villagers, their very affluence reminds them of their complicity in local political corruption.

Figure 24   The members of "Johanna's Band" (author's photograph)

GIOCHI SENZA FRONTIERE
(GAMES WITHOUT FRONTIERS)

Another perspective on local identity and modernity can be found in the ritual of Sasso's community games. During the summer of 1993 a group of three young entrepreneurs was given the mandate to manage Sasso's recreational center and put on a community event. The event was intended to help the grassroots economy and provide summer entertainment for the townsfolk.

The event that the entrepreneurs organized was called *"Giochi Senza Frontiere"* (Games Without Frontiers) and was held during ferragosto (mid-August, the peak vacation season in Italy). The contestants worked in teams and competed in playful or humorous events that required both physical strength and cultural knowledge. Over the course of a week, the teams battled to win high scores in everything from soccer to tug-of-war competitions. The games were modeled after a French television show broadcast across Europe in which teams from different countries competed for prizes. During most of the events, spectators were present to egg on the participants. There were seven teams in all, with ten members in each group. The teams had colorful names like *"I Velenos"* (The Poisonous Ones) and "Forza" (Courage). The team that I was a member of was given the English name "Johanna's Band" (figure 24). The organizers of the games, Gianna, Pia, and Umberto, planned, managed, and refereed the activities, except for the corrida (sketch), which was evaluated by a panel of other townsfolk.

The festivities opened with the water-bucket game, a race to collect the most water in the briefest time possible. The contestants lay on their backs in a row; each player would reach behind to pass a bucket filled with water to the person in front until the last player emptied the remaining water into a barrel. At the end of the game all the participants were sopping wet and doused in water. In this event the "novitiates" were all drenched in water and officially initiated into the week's proceedings.

Almost all of the events had a humorous component and placed the participants in slightly absurd situations. In the spaghettata (spaghetti meal), the everyday activity of eating pasta was transformed into a competitive exercise of speed, while the game of mock soccer became an amusing form of slapstick comedy. In the first activity, contestants sat next to each other at a counter with a bib and a fork while they tried to consume the largest quantity of pasta in a given amount of time; this ritual feasting overtly subverted the rules of etiquette and celebrated the pleasures of gluttonous excess. In the mad race to finish the endless servings of food, the players spilled pasta and soiled their faces with sauce as spectators applauded and laughed from the sidelines.

Italy's favorite pastime – soccer – was approached with a similarly vaudevillian sensibility. Playing in a slippery plastic pool filled with soapy water, the contestants contorted their bodies in order to maintain their balance. The much-respected game of physical dexterity and coordination became a study in uncoordinated limbs, collisions, and spectacular falls. The game was rendered even more difficult by penalty shots that allowed members of the opposing teams to throw buckets of water onto the players. Throughout the game the spectators mercilessly teased the participants and their feeble attempts to stay on solid footing.

In the "Name That Tune" game, people had to identify pieces of music as they ran back and forth across the tennis court. The difficulty in this exercise lay in accessing cultural knowledge and successfully completing the sprint before the music stopped playing. The master of ceremonies, a well-known singer in a local band called Brown Sugar, introduced the songs and arbitrated the event. Under the pressure to beat the clock, contestants unwittingly mangled the titles of well-known songs. The audience laughed hysterically at the malapropisms that uncontrollably leapt out of the mouths of flustered contestants as they frantically ran to reach their destinations. Here, the taken-for-granted knowledge of Italian popular song became elevated to the level of a valued skill. This event not only served to legitimize Italian trivia, it also provided a theatrical display of grace under pressure.

In these games, the quotidian is celebrated and turned on its head. While the mundane activity of eating pasta is exaggerated and parodied, the beloved sport of soccer is deliberately ridiculed. Similarly, the simple act of identifying popular songs is rendered unmanageable and chaotic. In this "topsy turvy world" (Babcock 1978), Sassani gather to watch members of their community treat respected cultural institutions with playful abandon and complete disregard for social convention. The burdens of daily life are temporarily suspended, and people can embrace the taboo-breaking pleasures of transgression and play. While these games parodied hoary symbols of Italian society, other games spoke to local attitudes about social change.

The most highly attended part of the games was the corrida (literally, Spanish bullfight), an event patterned after a television variety show in which entertainers performed sketches and were lauded or given the gong by a panel of judges. To warm up the audience for the event, a Neapolitan vacationer read a poem he composed about Sasso and its attractive thoroughfare,[4] while a second performer sang a pensive song by Francesco Guccini. Typically the corrida showcases dancing, singing, and humorous sketches, but, in these community games, the contestants performed entirely comedic material.

As a whole, the sketches satirized local personalities and alluded to current developments in the community. In the winning play, an actor skillfully imitated the distinctive voice of Sasso's mayor as he fielded questions from a "news reporter." My team's sketch, entitled "I Crocetti" (literally, little crossroads; a neighborhood in Sasso, see figure 25), poked fun at the mannerisms, styles of speech, and attitudes of the people who live in one of Sasso's oldest districts. The old-timers who assemble in the narrow streets are well known to the community, and the audience that evening immediately recognized the people upon whom we based our characters. Members of my group also thought that my doing a send-up of myself would amuse the crowd. After all, I had been studying the Sassano natives for several months, and I am sure that at some moments in my fieldwork I had made a nuisance of myself by asking too many questions. The part that was written for me developed into a good-natured parody, which I took in the spirit in which it was intended. Aside from suggesting that I use my own tape recorder as a prop, affecting an exaggerated American accent and declaring my character's interest in the courting rituals of Sassani, I did not play a huge role in composing the sketch. Marina was the one who came up with the

Figure 25   *I Crocetti* (the crossroads neighborhood in Sasso) (author's photograph)

idea for *I Crocetti*, and she was responsible for making sure that our costumes and dialogue were true to life. We rehearsed our scene once and left the rest to our improvisatory skills.

Our stage show was comprised of two female protagonists who were played by Riccardo, a stocky male student in his mid-twenties, and Marina, a small-statured woman who attends nursing school in Sasso. The silent older man was played by Pietro, a student in his mid-twenties who is also in nursing school. The roles of the tawdry women were played by Marco (a tall, husky man in his early thirties) and Salvatore (a shorter, more slender, high-school student). I played an American folklorist who is studying the sexual habits of Sassani. Riccardo is dressed in a snug-fitting grembiule (the traditional smock older women wear to do housecleaning or labor intensive work), while Marina wears *il lutto* and a black headscarf. Pietro quietly sits in a chair with a tailor-fitted Sunday suit and a hat. He occasionally leans against his cane and displays the demeanor of a man from an older generation. The older characters speak an exaggerated local dialect and use outdated expressions; their conversation is peppered with slang and expletives.

The sketch opens with a scene of Riccardo, Marina, and Pietro casually passing the time. As I walk by, I draw the attention of the old-timers who inquisitively ask me who I am. With a tape recorder in hand and exaggerated American accent, I respond by giving my mother's clan name, a traditional way of identifying lineage and character. Then the two garishly dressed women, played by Marco and Salvatore, walk on stage wearing miniskirts and tank tops. Shaking their heads in disbelief and reprimanding the women for their indecent appearance, Riccardo and Marina are visibly scandalized. As the hairy, muscular, scantily clothed "women" continue on their path, Riccardo and Marina reminisce about the strict moral codes that prevailed in their times. Marina admits to her prudishness by confessing that her husband has yet to see her naked. Riccardo chimes in with, "It's simply unthinkable [for a woman's husband to see her naked]." Pietro nods his head in silent support. The neighborhood women go on with a short exchange about husbands, cooking, female modesty, and sexual relations.

In this sketch, Sassani reflexively explore and negotiate the issues of local identity and modernity. An example of what Milton Singer called cultural performances, the corrida illustrates how public display events draw upon a repertoires of established knowledge and have the potential to bring any social actor into their orbits – including culture brokers such as journalists and ethnographers.

As they watch the show, Sassani recognize themselves in the cast of strange characters. This small enclave of people who live in *I Crocetti* represents a rapidly disappearing way of life in Sasso. Today, Sassani can laugh at quaint *di vecchio stampo* (old-fashioned ideas), even though these values pervade their present attitudes about gender, family, and sex. At the opposite end of the spectrum is my character. The Sassano audience immediately recognized the irony in my part and were amused by the ways in which I identified and capitalized on Italian stereotypes of Americans and my role in the town. While many Italians are respectful, or even envious, of America's wealth and power (as exemplified in the enormous popularity of *Beverly Hills 90210* and *The Young and the Restless* in Italy), they also see Americans as an uncivilized lot who lack the history and culture to know how to live well (see chapter 6). Playing on these ideas, the "American Fieldworker in Italy" character exemplified all the qualities of this stereotype. My parody Giovanna was wealthy enough to pursue unprofitable academic interests and yet was so uncivilized and stupid that she is forced to look to Italy for lessons in the arts of culture. The role of the American buffone (fool) is frequently used in the Italian mass media for comic relief. In fact, only a few weeks before the games I had seen a blond showgirl by the name of Heater Parisi play the part of the clueless American in a sketch on a well-known variety show. My portrayal of the displaced social scientist in search of the "primitive other," a satirical metacommentary on my occupational status within the community, combined television-inspired images of the socially inept professor such as that found in *Gilligan's Island* with a reflexive, Judy Holiday vision of strategic incompetence. To the local audience that evening I was the daughter of Nannine Fangiarilli, and they could fully appreciate the humor in my portrayal of the linguistically impaired outsider. To the visitors from abroad and even my kinfolk, I was in many ways the byproduct of postwar emigration, an immigrant daughter who had come back to turn her anthropological gaze upon an other to which she had longstanding ties.

In sum, our corrida sketch parodies all of the participants in the Sassano social world, and neither the modern nor premodern are spared. With their outdated language, older Sassani are antiquated traditionalists with customs that are both prudish and vulgar. Depicted by the cross-dressing Marco and Salvatore, today's generation of women is sexually promiscuous and blurs the boundary between male and female roles. Finally, America is represented as a source of crass wealth and cultural ignorance and therefore serves as an icon of corrupted modernity. Unlike the reversible world of the spaghet-tata and the mock soccer game, the corrida expresses and exaggerates the attitudes that Sassani have about social change.

While most of the games at the polisportivo provided a means of commenting upon contemporary social life in Sasso, the *caccia agli oggetti* (treasure hunt) involved the pursuit of the obscure, yet find-able past. Unlike a conventional treasure hunt, the contestants had to find people as well as objects. As a result, this event involved the full participation of the community.

Within the fenced-in tennis court of the recreation center, players from the ten groups gathered and were handed a list of items to find.

1 *Portare una pecora.* (Bring a sheep.)
2 *Una moneta da L100 e una da L50 dell'anno 1960.* (100 and 50 lire pieces from 1960.)
3 *Due componenti della squadra devono vestirsi con abiti nuziali. (Sposo e sposa) non è importante il sesso di chi si veste.* (Two members must come dressed as bride and groom; the sex of the members who wear these costumes is unimportant.)
4 *Un componente deve vestirsi da militare.* (A team member must get dressed as a military officer.)
5 *Trovare una copia del "Corriere della sera" del giorno 10–08–93.* (Find a copy of the newspaper from 10 August 1993.)
6 *Trovare la persona più pesante e la più leggera dai 35 anni in su.* (Find the heaviest and lightest person older than thirty-five years of age.)

7 *Portare un calzolaio.* (Bring a cobbler.)
8 *Portare una protesi totale (dentiera).* (Bring a set of dentures.)
9 *Portare una foto di Papa Paolo vi.* (Bring a photo of Pope Paul vi.)
10 *Portare un suonatore di "ddu botte" con relativo brano da eseguire.*
(Bring a *ddu botte* player; the musician will be expected to play a
verse.)

*Dagli organizzatori: nell'augurare in bocca al lupo raccomandiamo molta
prudenza per la buona riuscita del gioco. Pronti, via! ...* (From the organizers: We wish you the best of luck and the successful completion
of this game. On your mark, get set, go ...)

As soon as the organizers finished explaining the rules, the participants quickly discussed a game plan and disbanded; a flurry of cars
exited the center.

From the outset, our team hedged our bets by focusing our energies
on the objects that we were certain to find. From my aunt's house we
made phone calls and divided up our forces. Pietro went home to get
his dad's old military outfit. Marina and I went to the newspaper
store to look for the back issue of *Corriere della Sera*, while Riccardo
went looking for the local shoe store owner and brought along his
father's extra set of dentures. Within the span of approximately forty
minutes, we began to make our way back to *il polisportivo*.

Many Sassani watched the commotion from afar and laughed at the
comical, desperate efforts of the participants. The processional march
of cars on the way to the center created a festive atmosphere, and the
town buzzed with activity. The participants pooled their resources for
the massive search and had to agree upon the best plan of action.
Strategy and speed were of essence to this part of the game. The spectators who watched the proceedings from their balconies, stoops, and
cars were highly amused by the antics of the players. This purposeful
activity injected a jolt of energy and excitement into an otherwise lazy
Sunday afternoon in Sasso. The players who scurried about the piazza
on that day were a veritable vision of youthful exuberance, industry,
and ingenuity. In many ways, these task-oriented minions are a
testament to the power of human creativity. Here, consumers are
transformed into producers with the power to act and affect the world.
These performances, however, also provide a playful parody of the
work ethic by celebrating the non-instrumental goals of pleasure.

Back at the polisportivo, the players started to trickle in wearing
retro wedding gowns and ill-fitting military outfits. The cast of strangely
dressed characters gave the event a slightly surreal quality. With
bleating sheep and the last *ddu botte* player in Sasso, this motley crew
of people looked like a misplaced caravan of theater performers.

Whether or not the architects of the games intended it, the effect of the treasure hunt was to produce a spectacle of antiquated Sassani artifacts and, by decontextualizing these objects, to illustrate their very distance from contemporary Sassano life. Here, Sassani playfully look back at aspects of their culture that have almost disappeared. The remaining emblems of this old way of life, however, are looked upon with humor and irony instead of longing and dread. Within the context of the treasure hunt, Sassani made light of their ambivalent attitudes toward modernity; they laughed at themselves and their historical predicament. As a result, the process of social change was made less daunting. In a list of everyday objects and people from Sasso's past, the village's last *ddu botte* player, sheep, and cobbler stand out as an image of another era. They are anachronistic reminders of the past; quaint cultural survivals that look out of place in the modern world of Sassano society. The fear of change that Sassani expressed to me in the interviews, however, was absent in this event. Safely ensconced in the ritual frame, people playfully pay homage to the last vestiges of their pastoral roots and are poised to embrace their modern identities.

Despite the overall levity of Sasso's *Giochi Senza Frontiere*, a highly contestatory attitude permeated the games from the outset. The judging of the teams prompted jeers and responses from the crowd, especially if participants chose to interpret the conditions broadly. For example, during the treasure hunt, the most hotly debated item on the list was number seven, the cobbler. With the rise of cheap, disposable consumer goods there was only one person left in the town who actually repaired shoes. The rules, however, did not provide any definition of the word, and, as a result, several arguments broke out. Our team brought with us Mr Scarpa, a local shoe store owner who, in theory, repairs shoes, but in practice sends most of his work to other people. Some of the other players were up in arms about our choice and tried to convince the organizers that Mr Scarpa did not meet the criteria. A semantic discussion about the meaning of the word calzolaio (cobbler) ensued and various players disagreed over the merits of the players arguments. After a rambunctious deliberation on the topic, the organizers decided to concede us our points.

Beyond this particular conflict, the players were extremely competitive. They frequently challenged the authority of the organizers and fiercely criticized each other for their lack of fair play. At almost every stage of the games, especially early on when tempers were heated, participants accused opponents of cheating and carefully monitored their performances. While some of this behavior was done in the spirit of fun, these antics often caused disruptive outbursts of anger.

After being berated repeatedly for failing to penalize players who were bending the rules, one of the organizers got on the microphone and told everybody, "*Andate tutti a fanculo*" (Go fuck yourselves).

The players felt that the judges failed to be vigilant in their role as official arbitrators of the event. They were also frustrated with their competitors failure to comply with the rules. Many of the participants felt that this lack of sportsmanship forced otherwise honest players to resort to dishonest means in order to stay in the game. The common assumption among the participants was that people will cheat, which in turn pressured others to resort to trickery. In this context, the challenge of the games lies in obfuscating the rules rather than playing according to them. Following instructions essentially meant jeopardizing your chances of winning. In this situation, Sassani ultimately have to choose between *passare per fessi* (passively being made the fool) or *prendere gli altri per fessi* (actively taking others for fools).

The discord that prevailed in the games was also present in the management of the polisportivo. The three people who planned and organized the events had their share of disagreements about running the business equitably and profitably. There were numerous arguments about questionable bookkeeping practices, refereeing responsibilities, and the allotment of tasks. These antagonisms reached their peak at the end of the season when it came time to divide the earnings from the summer's business enterprise.

While the conflict among organizers could have happened in any small business, the combative rhetorical style of the contestants is, perhaps, more suggestive. The players' strategies of interaction (constantly challenging the terms of debate, attacking the opponents as a means of defense) and their social predicament as competitors in the game (being forced to cheat to stay in the competition) are not unlike those of any disadvantaged actor in any corrupt social system. Here, the parallels between the ritual competition and the real world are all too obvious. In the context of pervasive institutionalized corruption, even the most virtuous have to pay bribes to make their way in the world. In the context of a Byzantine, corrupt, and all-pervasive bureaucracy, the skills of discussione (a genre of verbal debate; see Corsaro 1988, 1990, 1994) are fundamental to one's social survival. Among any people historically conditioned to distrust authority, individual actors will feel compelled to do battle with the status quo and look for ways of subverting the establishment. Strategies of wit and shrewdness are the only weapons of defence for people who lack power.

Over the centuries, central Italy has been dominated by a wide variety of groups, and, to a large degree, the legacy of this foreign domination is the contemporary system of raccomandazioni and corruption. In this perverse world, menefreghismo (couldn't carelessism) is an attitude that many contemporary Italians adopt to debunk, and to resist, the myth that they are living in a liberal democracy. If one considers this larger social context, Sassani's lack of respect for organized institutions beyond the family is more comprehensible. I see the defensive posture that some participants adopted during the games as a survival strategy, rather than as evidence of the uncivic mindedness that some social scientist have attributed to Italians (Lemann 1995). Understood in this way, combativeness is driven by self-preservation instead of an active desire to harm others.[5] These small acts of resistance ultimately allow Sassani to reclaim a semblance of freedom and autonomy from the state. (In a related vein, see Barzini 1964; Romanucci-Ross 1991.)

In many ways, the *Giochi Senza Frontiere* draw together the various themes of this chapter. The audience's disgust with the players' combative style harkens back to Sassani's feelings of anger at the town's undemocratic politics. The players' predicament (being forced to cheat by the all-pervasive cheating of others, cheating as the very condition of participation) echoes the situation of any Sassani confronting the local system of patronage and raccomandazioni. By the same token, the moments of conviviality and pleasure that the games provided speak to the sense of pride Sassani feel about their town and the genuine benefits that development has brought. The polisportivo itself reflects their situation; it is both a home to Sasso's rituals of community and a reminder of the town's political connections. The surreal display of antiquated artifacts in the new polisportivo is a fitting image of the contradictions of modernity.

4

The Miracle, the Blonde, and the Prostitutes: Gender and Social Change in Sassano Discourse

While the previous chapter examined Sassano interpretations of the political and economic dimensions of modernity, this chapter focuses on changing gender roles. Discussing a national media event, a popular soap opera, and a controversial Sassano scandal, I will explore the wide range of perspectives that the townsfolk have on gender in contemporary Italian society and how their perspectives are informed by generation and class. Building on the previous chapter, I will also suggest how gender issues play themselves out in the larger discourses about modernity and local identity.

In today's Sasso, gender roles are in flux. Traditionally, women in rural central Italy were relegated to the domestic life and expected to perform the duties of wife and mother, while the public sphere was reserved for men. This gendering of public and private was justified by local beliefs about sexuality in which women were seen to possess a nearly overwhelming sexual power – a power that they, the women, had the unfortunate responsibility of policing. Athough there were situations in which cross-gender interaction was common, for women to appear in public alone could be read as a sexually provacative act, and women felt a strong social pressure to observe rules of decorum and modesty. While some vestiges of these attitudes still remain in Sasso today, much has changed. Young women appear in public and date without chaperones, and a small group of local women have pursued careers in business. Further, almost all of the townsfolk would, when asked, affirm their belief in gender equality, though the situation on the ground is more complex. Childrearing and domestic work are still common expectations for Sassano women. They feel a special presure to marry, and the sexual promiscuity of men is tolerated much more than that of women. (For more background on the gender roles in Sasso, see chapter 1.)

LOCAL RESPONSES TO THE
DISAPPEARANCE OF YLENIA

In early January of 1994, Ylenia Carrisi, the daughter of the famous Italian singing duo Al Bano and Romina Power, disappeared while travelling in the United States. After spending a few months in Belize, Ylenia made her way to New Orleans, where she was last seen walking with an African-American street musician called Alexander Masakela. Al Bano and Power searched relentlessly for their daughter, and hardly a day went by in 1994 without a broadcast or a headline about Ylenia's disappearance. Everyone in Sasso was acquainted with the affair and had an opinion to share on the topic. In this section, I will examine what the responses to the Ylenia story tell us about modernizing gender roles in Sassano culture. My discussion of Ylenia's disappearance is based upon data that I culled from Italy's national press, while my discussion of local responses to the affair was gleaned from interviews, casual conversation, and daily interactions with the townsfolk in Sasso.

Italy's national media covered the story of Ylenia's disappearance extensively; these reports represent the most traditional construction of Italian gender roles. Drawing on European stereotypes of America, the television networks portrayed scenes of sleazy bars and strip clubs along Canal and Bourbon Streets. Even the widely respectable magazine *Panorama* sensationalized the affair. One headline ran:

Anatomia del giallo di New Orleans. Ylenia dei misteri. I giorni con "Mescal." Il giro del voodo. L'attrazione per un mondo nero. L'inviato di "Panorama" racconta come si perde una ragazza perbene.

Anatomy of a mystery in New Orleans. Ylenia of mystery. Days with "Mescal." The circle of voodoo. The attraction of the Black world. In this article, a reporter tells *Panorama* how a girl from a good family is lost (De Martino 1994, 15).

In the article, journalist Marco De Martino traces Ylenia Carrisi's fascination with travel and disenfranchised street folk to the novels of Jack Kerouac and the beat writers. One particularly melodramatic sidebar reads, "*Ylenia Carrisi è andata a New Orleans per seguire la sua hero America da On the Road e la generazione dei beat. Ecco cosa ci rimane oggi."* (Ylenia Carrisi went to New Orleans to follow her hero America from *On the Road* and the beat generation. This [her disappearance] is the result.) However, it is in the representation of Masakela, Ylenia's alleged lover, that the depictions of urban decay and witchcraft are fully elaborated.

In the Italian media, Masakela emerged as an alluring New Age Svengali with a loyal flock of female devotees. A spiritual guru, street musician, and ladies' man, he is described as having a charismatic personality. Ylenia called him "master" in her travel notebook, the papers said. In a regional Abruzzese newspaper, *Il Centro*, Al Bano reportedly describes Masakela as the *"'spirito del male'* (an evil spirit), with eyes that can hypnotize and incite fear" (Visconti 1994, 7). According to the *Panorama* article, Masakela's name means "devil" in Creole (De Martino 1994, 16). In this eight-page, photo-illustrated piece, the author dwells upon Masakela's alleged links to Satanism and describes New Orleans as a town terrorized by "The Circle," a Satanic cult that specializes in human sacrifice. De Martino explains that:

Qui si ricorda che nel 1969 arrivò in città un gruppo di seguaci di Anoton Szender Le Vey, l'autore della Bibbia satanica: venivano dalla California dove uno di loro, Charles Manson, si è appena messo nei guai con la strage nella vita dell'attrice Sharon Tate. Per un po' diedero vita ad un culto legale: poi entrarono nella clandestinità.

Here, let us remember that in 1969, the followers of Anton Szendor Le Vey, author of the *The Satanic Bible*, came to New Orleans to establish themselves as a legal religion; after, they went underground. One of this groups most famous members was the notorious Charles Manson, who helped plan the Sharon Tate murder in California (De Martino 1994, 12).

One of the main themes in the news reports was how the golden couple of Italian song were forced to interact with the worst element of New Orleans society. This flashy headline from *Panorama* describes the couple's descent into the eerie underworld of the French Quarter: *"L'Odissea di Romina e Al Bano nei bassifondi"* (The Odyssey of Romina and Al Bano in the Underbelly of New Orleans). According to L. Ann's article in *Corriere della sera*, the parents desperate search for their daughter led the celebrity couple to seek out help from a variety of mediums, witnesses, and even a powerful Mafia family in New Orleans.

What is most interesting, perhaps, about the Ylenia story is that the American-born mother is almost always blamed for her daughter's fate. While reporters cast the father in the role of strict Southern disciplinarian, the American-born mother is assigned to play the indulgent, hippy parent. In the press, Romina Power's past life is moralistically recounted for the public's pleasure. The daughter of Hollywood actor Tyrone Power and Scandinavian model Linda Christian, Romina Power had reportedly been a rebellious teenager with a penchant for outrageous Mary Quant clothes and a fast crowd of iconoclastic foreign friends. De Martino states that:

Lei è una ragazzina molto chiacchierata, molto carina, molto "swinging London." Veste Mary Quant e si fa vedere in giro con il figlio di Balthus, eccentrico ragazzo magro e altissimo, principe con inclinazione hippy.

She [Romina] is a much talked about girl, very pretty and very "swinging London." She wears Mary Quant fashions and goes around town with the son of Balthus, a tall, eccentric prince with hippy inclinations (De Martino 1994, 15).

The author goes on to describe Romina's torrid romance with Al Bano, a man eleven years her senior. The report represents her as a precocious, jet-setting seventeen-year-old who was finally saved from her shallow existence by the love of an older man. In De Martino's representation, Romina is a rootless young woman who finds the stability and warmth she longs for in her husband's extended family in Celline San Marco. De Martino explains that:

È la figlia di Tyrone Power e di una svitata come Linda Christian. L'ambiente della madre, ore piccole ed esaurimenti nervosi, non le piace. Non le piace nemmeno il mondo del cinema. Cresciuta fra rigore dei college inglesi e disordine materno, cerca qualcosa di solido, cerca radici ... Fugge dall'immagine di ninfetta che le era stata cucita addosso.

She [Romina] is the daughter of Tyrone Power and the nutcase, Linda Christian. She doesn't care for her mother's lifestyle, late hours, and nervous break-downs. Neither does she like the world of the cinema. Brought up between a restrictive English boarding school and disordered, absent mother, she seeks something solid, she seeks roots ... She flees the nymphet image into which she was cast (De Martino 1994, 16).

Later on in the article, the American-born Romina is blamed for failing to provide her Italian daughter with the proper maternal guidance. In both cases, the sins of the mothers (Linda Christian and Romina Power) are visited upon the daughters (Romina Power and Ylenia Carrisi). While the young Romina is saved from her hedonistic life, her daughter Ylenia falls victim to the same desires for adventure and excitement. Throughout their articles, reporters from *Panorama* and *Corriere della sera* subtly praised the authoritarian character of the Italian father, while the American mother is condemned for her indulgent, liberal-minded parenting and her checkered past.

The media depictions of the Ylenia affair draw upon conservative ideas about gender and modernity in Italian culture. The story is represented as a cautionary tale in which the protagonist is punished for her transgression of traditional gender roles and her modern desire for pleasure and self-fulfillment. Italian images of America are crucial here. As I suggested in the previous chapter, Italians often represent America as the site of corrupt modernity, a place where industrialization has led to a blurring of gender boundaries and therefore a moral decline. In line with these notions, the young American Romina becomes an image of all that is wrong with modern women; sexually promiscuous, she lacks a moral compass and must be redeemed by a strong patriarchic from the South – the region most closely associated with traditional Italy. Similarly, Ylenia's desire for freedom and autonomy leads her to corruption and disaster. In Italy, she is an innocent little girl who can be protected by the strong hand of her father. When the protections (read: constraints) of the Italian family are allowed to lapse by a permissive mother, Ylenia is inevitably drawn to America, the site of modernity and decadence. In this view, women are weak, men are strong, and anyone who fails to observe traditional gender roles is subject to the evils of the world.

Local responses to these media representations varied by generation and gender and highlighted the differing perspectives on women's roles found in Sasso. The conversation at my aunt's dinner table one weekday afternoon can serve as an introduction. On that day, the television blared yet another news report on the Ylenia story, and my uncle, a man of few words, was moved to speak. Sighing, he waived his hand in the air and said, "*È una povera drogata; tante storie ...*" (She's a drug addict. I don't understand the fuss ...) Cousin Amelio chimes in, "*Che è andata a fare a New Orleans prima di tutto? Perchè non è rimasta a casa invece di trattare con cattiva gente?*" (Why did she go to New Orleans in the first place? Why didn't she stay home, instead of hanging out with those loathsome characters?) I replied, "*Se fosse stato un uomo non vi saresti posti la domanda. Forse era una ragazza giovane piena di idealismo e curiosità che è caduta in un giro di cose che sono andate fuori controllo?*" (If she had been a man you wouldn't be asking the question. She was bright and curious – perhaps an idealistic teenager who got involved in things that got out of her control?) Amelio gave me the fish eye. His mind was made up. His silence spoke volumes, and his facial expression suggested that Ylenia was a promiscuous adventurer who ultimately got what she deserved.

Figure 26   Key participants in the "Ylenia" conversation; left to right: Rosa,
Patrizia, Amelio, and Massimo (author's photograph)

My aunt Norina turned to me and said, "*Quello che non capisco è
perchè ha passato la notte con quel brutto. Era un brutto vagabondo.*"
(I don't understand why she spent the night with that awful-looking
man. He was a dirty vagabond.) "*Può darsi che abbiano solo condiviso
la camera*" (Perhaps they just shared a room together), I replied. With
his cupped hands shaking backing and forth in disbelief, Amelio
interjected, "*Ma che!*" (I don't buy it!) "*Forse è sparita; New Orleans é
una città con uno dei più alti tassi di criminalità negli Stati Uniti*" (She
could just have gone missing; New Orleans has one of the highest
crime rates in the United States), said Massimo, a university student
in his early twenties. Uninterested in the affair, Rosa, a nurse in her
early thirties, said, "*Si è probabilmente buttata nel fiume e dovranno
aspattare che venga a galla; hanno detto che hanno visto una ragazza che
assomigliava a lei.*" (She probably threw herself in the river like that
witness claims. We won't know until the river dredges her up, but
they said that they saw a woman who fit her description.) With mock
disdain, Patrizia, another young woman, added, "*È stata rapita e
venduta come schiava*" (She was kidnapped and sold into White
slavery). Patrizia's mother Gabriella said, "*Che dispiacere!*" (What
sorrow!). In a dismissive tone, Amelio asked, "*Perchè non è rimasta a
casa?*" (Why didn't she stay at home?). (See figure 26 for a photogragh
of the key participants in this conversation.)

   This one scene provides a snapshot of the sentiments that the
Ylenia case elicited in Sasso, and it illustrates how Sassani's responses
varied according to gender and age. As we will see, the older women
in the community usually failed to comprehend Ylenia's attraction to
a poor, disreputable man of color who made a living as an itinerant
street musician. In the photo layouts and television footage, these
Sassano women saw a disheveled, shabbily dressed middle-aged
man with penetrating eyes and long hippy dreads. The older men
were far more critical of Ylenia's desire for autonomy and sexual
freedom. The younger people with whom I interacted were nonchalant
about Ylenia's alleged indiscretions and her search for excitement in
faraway places.

   The women in their mid-fifties or sixties with whom I spoke routinely wondered aloud about Ylenia's motives for sharing a hotel
room with a homeless bohemian drifter. For example, one woman
said, "*Cosa stava facendo con quello? Non era un bell'uomo. Mi sembra
un brutto zozzone con quella barba.*" (What was she doing with him; he
wasn't a nice-looking man. He looks like a dirty bum with that
beard.) Others asked, "*Cosa vedeva in lui?*" (What did she see in him?).
They could not fathom why a pretty, well-educated woman like
Ylenia would get involved with an indigent man twice her age. In
these women's eyes, Masakela defied the rules of sexual attraction.
They simply failed to understand how the man from the photographs
could have seduced the "*bella bionda*" ("lovely young blonde"). In
their opinion, this ill-kempt "*zozzone*" (dirty bum) with the scruffy
beard did not constitute *un buon partito* (a good catch, a good prospect).
For this female cohort Masakela was the antithesis of a desirable son-
in-law, and we can use their reactions to him to understand their
vision of respectability and marriageability. Masakela not only failed
to be traditionally handsome, he was lacking in other qualities that
would make him an appropriate marriage partner – wealth, gracious-
ness, sophistication, and respectability. Represented as a sinister-
looking bohemian by the Italian popular press, Masakela seemed to
lead a life unconstrained by the bourgeois values of work, family,
and material success, and, as such, he posed a threat to the normative
values of Sassano society. Contextualized by narratives and discourses, it was visual images of Masakela that were indicators of his
unsuitability for this older generation of Sassano women, and in
chapter 5 I will explore how values like reputation, respectability, and
marriageability are displayed through visual and bodily means.

   Ultimately, it is Masakela's race that makes him unsuitable for the
pretty and "well-bred" Ylenia Carrisi. Although, it was never explicitly stated, it is clear that some of the women with whom I spoke did

not approve of the liaison between an African-American man and a White woman. While Catholic strictures against premarital sex still hold sway among the older generation of Sassani, the prejudices against interracial relationships seem to be even stronger. In the context of these ideas, Ylenia committed a double sin: she violated the Church's prohibitions against sex before marriage and transgressed the confines of race by having an affair with a man of color. In so doing, Ylenia became sexually impure and racially polluted. Within the urban environment of corrupt American modernity, traditional boundaries (be they of race or gender) are blurred and always with disastrous results.

These same older women would often focus on Ylenia's tender age and inexperience. They believed she was a young innocent who fell prey to the hostile forces of the street. *"Forse l'hanno drogata o intrappolata"* (Maybe they drugged her or she fell into a trap), one woman said. Married women with children of their own frequently expressed sympathy for Al Bano's and Power's sorrows. They often exclaimed, *"Povera ragazza; tanti dispiaceri per i genitori"* (Poor girl; so much sorrow for her parents). While the older women couldn't understand Ylenia's attraction to Masakela and condemned her relationship with him, only one directed angry or derisive comments at Ylenia herself, accusing her of being "sciocca" (careless, lacking in common sense).

Even younger Sassano women identified with the couple's anguish. For example, one Sassano school teacher in her late thirties, Amalia, was particularly struck with the dissonance between the singing duo's carefree tunes and the tragic loss of their daughter. In the popular imagination, Al Bano and Power are most often rememberd for their career-defining performance of "Felicità" ("Happiness"), which occurred many years ago at the San Remo song festival (a widely televised song competition and one of Italy's best-known cultural institutions). Clearly in love with one another, the two performed a song that celebrated the simple joys of *un panino* and *un bicchiere di vino* ("a sandwich" and "a glass of wine"). This image is in jarring opposition to that of the grieving parents, which the media covered so extensively during my fieldwork. For Amalia, "Felicità" now evokes deep sadness and reminds her of a happier period in the singers' career. She said, *"Adesso quando sentirò la canzone mi ricorderò della loro povera figlia che è sparita, è molto triste"* (Now when I hear the song I'll remember their missing daughter; it is very sad). For Amalia, this optimistic tune of bright-eyed love and youthful exuberance now only smacks of misery and pain.

Unlike most of the women with whom I spoke, the older men expressed little sympathy for the plight of the missing "girl"; they believed that she paid the price for associating with *la mala vita* (criminals and thieves who live on the fringe of society). On several occasions I heard the habitues of the corner bar say, "*È una sbandata senza giudizio*" (She's a wreckless person with no common sense). One man said, "*Cosa stava facendo lì da sola, non riesco a capire*" (What she was doing there alone, I don't understand). These men frequently had nothing but scorn for "*questo genere di ragazza*" (this kind of girl) and "*la sua vita spericolata*" (life without fear). They felt that she had succumbed to her own misplaced desires for adventure and excitement. By straying away from the safety of the home, Ylenia had challenged the gender expectations of traditional Italian society. Her "libertine" attitudes not only threaten the dictates of Catholic morality but the patriarchal ideas that once defined Sassano culture.

The younger people in Sasso were generally less judgmental about Ylenia's lifestyle; they never accused her of being promiscuous or irresponsible. To many Sassani in their late teens and early twenties, she was merely a victim of foul play. As one young woman said, "*Poteva succedere pure qui [Italy]. Ogni giorno sparisce la gente. Succede dappertutto.*" (It could have happened even here [in Italy]. People disappear everyday. It happens everywhere.) Another said, "*Tra tutta quella droga, prostitute e ladri qualsiasi cosa può accadere*" (Among the drugs, prostitutes, thieves, any number of things could have happened to her). The young people I knew were neither shocked nor scandalized by what happened. In fact many were completely indifferent to the case.

On the local level, responses to the Ylenia affair highlight differing perspectives on women's roles in Italian culture. In traditional Italian society, women were discouraged from travel, work outside of the home, and the broad range of activities that today are associated with personal autonomy and fulfillment. Up to the 1950s, the practice of forced seclusion was in place, and women were often discouraged from leaving the home unchaperoned; those who did were thought to be promiscuous and brought dishonor to the family name (Del Negro 1997). Like the media reports, the comments of Sasso's older men depict Ylenia's disappearance as the inevitable result of transgressing these traditional restrictions. Sasso's older women, however, subtly rejected the narrowly defined views of gender and sexual morality. In everyday exchanges about the event, Sassano women generally refrained from passing judgment on Ylenia's honor. They saw no harm in the young woman's desire to broaden her experience and see the world. Comparing the various commentaries, it is clear that the older Sassano men were far more invested in the notion of female chastity. The young people I spoke with in Sasso, however, were considerably less punitive about Ylenia's interest in travel. While they thought that she may have exercised poor judgment, they did not blame her for her unconventional lifestyle.

That older men should be invested in a system of gender relations that justifies the domination and control of the women is not difficult to understand. Similarly, that the older women should be less committed to these kinds of interpretation is also intuitive. The situation, however, is more complex than it initially seems. In the comments of the older women, I detect an implicit sympathy for the striving for greater personal options that their daughters seek and perhaps even a dim memory of their own youthful longings. While in no way denying the oppressive sexism of the older men's interpretation, one can observe a perverse vulnerability in their position. In traditional Italian society, the man's honor is something that is at least partially out of his hands; it depends on the activities of his wife and daughters. While the sexist control of women and the practices of forced seclusion are in no way justified by the men's feeling of powerlessness, their domination of women comes from the inherently untenable position into which these men have been thrust. Sympathizing with the shame that Ylenia brought to her father, their judgmental attitude toward her is as much a comment on their own powerlessness as it is evidence of their repressive attitudes toward women. Unable to see modernized gender roles as liberating to both men and women, the older Sassano males see women's newfound freedoms as a further erosion of the already tenuous control they have over their own social identities.

MILAGROS

If the experiences of older men in Sasso provide insights into Italian gender roles, the lives of Sasso's older, working-class women are equally instructive. Their experiences are unique in Sasso, and, in many ways, this group has seen the fewest benefits from the social changes that modernity has wrought. With varying degrees of acceptance and resistance, all of the older women of Sasso have been informed by traditional Catholic notions of womanhood. Born before the Second World War, they are too old to have taken advantage of the broadened gender roles that younger Sassano women enjoy. Whether they view the women of the postwar generation with scorn or longing, those of the previous generation cannot fully share in the newfound freedoms. Further, older working-class women have reaped the least economic benefit from Sasso's industrialization. While they have known the pleasures of child-rearing and the domestic life, they look out at today's society and see images of gender and class progress that they know they will never directly experience. Perched between the present and the past, they have been doubly marginalized by modernity.

Making the rounds of shops and homes in Sasso, I quickly learned that the Argentinean television series *Milagros* had a loyal following among this group. Every Wednesday evening, they tuned their televisions to Channel 4 to enjoy this two-hour telenovela. While a cross-section of Sasso's population was familiar with *Milagros*, its most ardent followers were older, working-class women from the ages of fifty to eighty who spent their time tending to older relatives and grandchildren and preparing meals for their extended families. Mostly married or widowed, these homemakers work hard to maintain filial ties and diligently use their skills, resources, and knowledge to help with household expenditures. They are the unremunerated members of the hidden economy – those whose invisible work, efforts, and competence often goes unrecognized by society (Smith 1987).

At first, I believed that watching *Milagros* was a trivial pastime, and I had little enthusiasm for the hours that awaited me if one of my research participants was to invite me to spend a Wednesday evening at her home. Shows like *Milagros* were not unknown to me. RAI International is a television network that aired programs from the Italian state broadcasting company to a variety of foreign media markets, and in the late 1980s my parents began to watch this station on cable television in Montreal. Weekly telenovelas were a big part of the evening programing on RAI International, and my mother was devoted to these shows. Her friends would gather in our TV room, and their fascination with every twist and turn of the Byzantine plots bordered on the fanatical. A graduate student returning home from breaks and vacations, I could never understand my mother's attachment to these programs. In my feminist disdain, I found them to be maudlin and fatalistic, endlessly reinforcing patriarchal images of women. My mother would have been pleased if I drank coffee and nibbled Savoiarde biscuits (Italian ladyfinger cookies) while she and her friends learned if this week, finally, Maria would realize that the lecherous Giuseppe had been unfaithful, but at the time I simply could not bear these shows. When they came on, I would either go out with my friends or, if my mother was alone, stay home and read *Il cittadino canadese* (an Italian immigrant weekly) on a distant corner of the couch.

When I went to Sasso for my research, I was not surprised that the telenovelas were popular, but neither was I eager to study them. Many Sassano homes do not have a North American–style family room or den; instead a small couch and television is typically placed in the kitchen and that room is used for both food preparation and TV-viewing. Sitting one evening in the kitchen of Carmelina, one of the older, working-class Sassani whom I interviewed, my mind was not fully engaged by the telenovela *Milagros*, and I began to think about Janice Radway's *Reading the Romance* (1984), a path-breaking study of a romance-novel reading group in the US. Radway begins her book by summarizing a widely cited interpretation of Harlequin romance literature by Tania Modeleski, a well-known feminist critic. Modeleski reads these novels as gender ideology. Though these narratives might imagine women in the roles of doctors or lawyers, Modelski argues, they ultimately depict women as passive recipients of male sexual advances and normalize traditional patriarchal institutions, especially marriage and childrearing. Taking the social act of reading, rather than the text alone, as her focus, Radway worked closely with a group of women who read these novels and tried to understand the function that they played in their lives. While cognizant of the potentially regressive impact of these texts, Radway argued that the interpretations of cultural critics could be enhanced by exploring the situated contexts of audience reception and the creative interpretations that those readers might make. The result of her reader response method was a rich, three-dimensional interpretation that was no less feminist then Modeleski's, and her work has been a beacon for a generation of scholars. Watching *Milagros* in Carmelina's kitchen, the feminist criticisms of my earlier years rang in one ear, but Radway's methodological warnings to seek out participant perspectives rang in the other. It was only after many months of fieldwork that I began to realize that these shows might offer an entrance into the experience of older Sassano women.[1]

The story of *Milagros*, dubbed in Italian, is set in turn-of-the century South America and revolves around a young woman named Milagros (Spanish for "miracles") who struggles to become reunited with her long lost mestizo lover. Throughout the series, Milagros becomes embroiled in a string of ill-fated events that test her honor, virtue, and perseverance. Despite her trials, Milagros remains steadfast in her female chastity, her Catholic faith, and her fidelity to her absent partner. Across the span of the series, she fends off her evil stepbrother's sexual advances and desperately tries to evade the unkind and malicious strangers who cross her path. In one episode she is duped into joining a brothel and is saved from a tragic end by a sympathetic prostitute.

The experience of watching *Milagros* in the Italian home is an active one. The actors in the series are well known in Italy, and families all over Sasso discussed the episodes and bantered about the gyrations of the plot. The women with whom I watched the program identified with the protagonist's circumstances and shared a special kinship with her. A modern-day Madonna figure, she was deeply admired for her courage and elicited an almost religious devotion from her fans. As we will see, this character's troubled life parallels the trials and tribulations of female Catholic martyrs. In the face of rapid social change, this pious vision of femininity valorizes suffering and provides a metaphor for understanding the social inequalities of class and gender. This traditional model of womanhood ultimately helps older, working-class Sassano women make sense of the social changes that they have experienced.

One of the reasons that *Milagros* is able to appeal to its fans is its well-known cast. As a genre, telenovelas usually employ nationally recognized writers, directors, and performers (Leal and Oliven 1988, 85). Grecia Colmenaris, the actress who plays Milagros, has acted in a large number of both evening and daytime series. The leading man, Osvaldo Laport, a performer not unlike Fabio in his appearance, is an established actor who also starred in a variety of successful shows. The director of this lavish program, Omar Romay, shares co-production credit with Silvio Berlusconi, a wealthy television mogul and Italy's current prime minister. Popular with Italians and a wide range of Latin Americans, *Milagros* draws on longstanding Catholic images and ideas about gender, and, distinct from American soap operas, it is part of a larger international, pan-Catholic media culture.

The women with whom I watched *Milagros* greatly admired the actress who played the leading role. Light-complected, with long, straight, auburn hair, a moon-shaped face, and an angelic smile, she bore an uncanny resemblance to Renaissance images of the Virgin Mary. This affinity was not lost on the Sassano women who would reverentially say, "*Sembra una Madonna*" (She looks like the Madonna). The dramatic close-up shots of celestial adoration and despair often reminded me of the stylized portraits of Maria Addolorata (Maria of the Sorrows) that I had seen in Italian churches throughout the country – including Sasso. In these depictions, Maria Addolarata is almost always seen pleading and her pain is clearly visible. This supplicating pose was frequently affected by the actress who played the lead role in *Milagros*.

In Catholicism, beauty and suffering are often essential to the attributes of female saints and martyrs. The theme of the fair and dutiful daughter who endures great misery is a leitmotif in Catholic folk legends. In keeping with this tradition, Milagros undergoes various forms of humiliation before she can achieve salvation. As

Kathy Figgen argues in *Miracles and Promises: Popular Religious Cults and Saints in Argentina*, "The physical subjection of the body to the pains and ordeals of ascetic discipline [is] an integrated part of sanctity" (Figgen 1990, 68). As the quintessential martyr, Milagros is continuously resisting rape and defending her chastity. The perils of sexual contact are omnipresent.

The Catholic pantheon is replete with the stories of victimized women who are praised for their courage and stamina in the face of adversity. In her book *One Hundred Towers* (1991), anthropologist Lola Romanucci-Ross describes the popularity in central Italy of such a martyr as Santa Rita. In the small town of Ascoli-Piceno, legend has it that after Santa Rita's abusive husband dies, she has a vision from God and enters a convent where she develops the gift to heal the sick and the infirm. The travails of Santa Rita are especially well known to the women of the town who hold her devotion to family and husband in high esteem.

In Argentina, one of the telenovela centers of the Spanish speaking world, writers have borrowed from the rich tradition of Catholic folk religion by adapting the stories of the saints for radio and television (Figgen 1990). Like *Milagros*, the popular folk legend *Defunta Correa* deals with a woman's search for her lost companion. Unlike Milagros, who is blissfully reunited with her partner, Correa is found dead with her newborn infant sucking her lifeless breast (Figgen 1990, 172). In both accounts, the heroines are recognized for their ability to "triumph over the demeaning circumstances of the feminine role" (Romanucci-Ross 1991, 123). Their characters are, in fact, defined by their abiding sacrifice and submission. While these legends clearly endorse gender inequities by promoting female compliance, they also speak of freedom from bondage and servitude and celebrate the power of divine intervention to restore justice in the world.

Class plays a prominent role in *Milagros*. The animosity between the landed aristocracy and the rural peasants in the show clearly resonated with many Sassano viewers. The women with whom I watched the telenovela identified with the character's humble origin; all of them were from modest, working-class backgrounds who themselves remember long hours of agricultural work. Crucial here is that, underneath her tattered clothes, Milagros is from a noble family. Unbeknownst to her mother, Milagros is switched at birth with her wicked aunt's illegitimate child. While she is raised by a poor but loving family of carnival entertainers, her cousin enjoys the benefits of affluence and respectability.

The ambiguity that we find in Milagros's class status is echoed in her Native American love interest. Of Spanish and Indian background,

Nathaniel also betrays his fine pedigree. Both noble savage and urban sophisticated intellectual, he writes popular novels under a pseudonym but is disqualified from enjoying the privileges of class and wealth by his racial background. While his marginal status excludes him from the world of comfort and power, it also frees him from the racist confines of the White man's world. Like Milagros, Nathaniel seeks the higher goals of truth and justice.

This theme of dual identity is crucial to the telenovela. The protagonist is not really a downtrodden peasant girl, but a member of the upper echelons of society; her boyfriend is not the savage that society believes him to be, but the child of a misbegotten love affair between a wealthy White man and a common Indian woman. Milagros and Nathaniel have a hidden virtue obscured by their assigned roles; these characters are larger and more complex than the labels society has placed upon them. Their commitment to honor and justice is the only outward sign of the nobility they hold within.

What is it about *Milagros* that resonated so deeply with my informants? Employing powerful imagery from the Catholic tradition, the *Milagros* telenovela allows Sassano women to make sense of the difficulties in their lives. They identified with Milagros's experiences of gender and class-based oppression, and her ultimate triumph gives them hope. The protagonist is a genteel aristocrat who appears to be a peasant; identifying with Milagros, the women ultimately transform their female and working-class status from a marker of social disadvantage into an almost mystical sign of inner nobility. Even the smallest indignity of everyday life becomes a reminder of hidden grace and a promise of eventual redemption.

It is not surprising then that these older Sassano women preferred the Latin-based telenovelas to the American-style soap operas such as *The Bold and the Beautiful* (broadcast in Italy under the English title *Beautiful*). The viewers of *Milagros* found little solace in the machinations of rich people who work in lavish corporate offices and commit adultery. The travails of a humble peasant girl vividly speak to these women's memories of the devastating effects of the Second World War and the oppressive class barriers of their youth. Identifying with Milagros, the women see her story as a confirmation of the values of nurturance, sexual chastity, and self-sacrifice – values whose transgression is the main theme of America's soap operas.

In sum, the soaps from the New World celebrate a decadent American modernity, while *Milagros* valorizes the tenets of traditional Catholic culture. If Sasso's older women do indeed look out at today's society and see images of gender and class progress that they know they will never enjoy, they also see pitfalls which they are glad they will never have to face. While they may envy the opportunities that young women have and the wealth of Italy's postwar middle class, they also see consumerism as shallow and the search for individual fulfillment as self-centered. Alienated from the benefits of modernity, they are both attracted to and repelled from this modern world that they constantly see but cannot possess. Ironically, it is *Milagros* – a product of the transnational, pan-Catholic media culture – that offers an alternative. *Milagros* celebrates a traditional Catholic ideology and provides a critique of modernity that both validates the women's experiences and gives meaning to their suffering.

SEXUAL SCANDALS: TWIN PEAKS AND THE DOWNTOWN BROTHEL RUMOR

If *Milagros* is a critique of the moral failures of modernity, then the Twin Peaks scandal was an object lesson in those failures. In the summer of 1993, the local police raided Sasso's only discotheque, an establishment with the English name "Twin Peaks." The club was the home of a drug and prostitution ring that employed underaged sex workers from foreign countries and criminal elements from Italy's "South." At the time of the controversial closing, the entire country was in a tailspin over the tangentopoli crisis and Sasso's mayor Lantenari was being investigated for peddling political influence. It is in the context of these political troubles that Twin Peaks must be understood.

When the scandal first broke, Sassani were outraged by the news. Even though none of the prostitutes' clients were jailed or even named in local media reports, their identities became common knowledge in Sasso. Many of the women with whom I spoke were pleased by this and felt that it was high time the community's philandering men got what they deserved. Adriana, a local shopkeeper, was one of the first to broach the topic with me. As I browsed her boutique, she casually leafed through the newspaper and explained how the Twin Peaks operation ran. Paraphrasing from the paper she said, *"durante la giornata era un luogo di ritrovo per i giovani, però durante le ore piccole si trasformava in casa a luci rosse"* (By day, the discotheque was a legitimate bar and by night a house of ill repute). *"Dicono che la mafia sia stata implicata"* (They think that the mafia might have been involved). In a mocking tone she said, *"Lo vedi cosa succede in questo paese morto. Ti ho detto che c'era un lato nascosto di Sasso."* (You see the things that happen in this dull town. I told you there is a subterranean, hidden side of Sasso.)

As we talked, Adriana questioned the accuracy of the newspaper account in *Il Centro*, which claimed that there were two thousand people present on the night of the raid. She also expressed doubts about the reported size of the sting operation, which, the paper maintained, involved twenty patrol cars and forty plainclothes policemen. Adriana took the scandal in stride and appreciated the entertainment value of this story. She kiddingly remarked, "*Aiuta a passare il tempo e togliermi la noia*" (It helps me to pass the time and break the tedium). Despite Adriana's lighthearted treatment of the affair, she admitted that she was pleased with the closure of the discotheque and glad to see the men who frequented the bar get their comeuppance.

My aunt Linda, a woman in her late sixties, was initially opposed to the construction of a discotheque in Sasso and was delighted when it was closed down. She believed that such establishments were unsavory and had a corrupting influence on the young – even without the drugs and prostitution. What she found most distasteful about the Twin Peaks affair was the exploitation of the underaged girls who had been smuggled in from Romania, the former Yugoslavia, and South America. She felt sorry for the teenage girls who were tricked into coming abroad with the hope of improving their lot. She said, "*Quelle povere ragazze che non hanno niente da mangiare e sono costrette a fare questo lavoro. È proprio triste.*" (These poor girls who haven't anything to eat and do this work. It is truly sad.)

The older women's condemnation of Twin Peaks was unintentionally given further impetus by the bar's name. The late-1980s American television series *Twin Peaks* was enormously popular in Italy. While, for Americans, the show drew upon the trope of the seamy underbelly of small-town life, for Italians, the show emphasized stereotypes of America that we have explored throughout – America as the site of a corrupt modernity. By naming the bar after David Lynch's series, the owners of the establishment hoped to invoke images of excitement and danger. With the subsequent prostitution scandal, the association of wealth, modernity, and uncontrolled sexuality was only drawn together more tightly.

While some Sassani feared the existence of a discotheque in their community, others looked favorably upon the idea. These people saw the establishment of a local disco as a sign of social progress, an emblem of their town's urban sophistication. When I first arrived in Sasso, people often boasted about the town's accomplishments by pointing to their recently built hospital and their very own discotheque. As a symbol of modernity, Twin Peaks represented the most lavish form of contemporary leisure that society could offer.

For many of the residents of the towns that neighbored Sasso, the Twin Peaks scandal was emblematic of Sassani's deeply flawed nature and moral depravity. In their eyes, Twin Peaks was the perfect marriage of corrupt Sassano politics and the world of crime. It exposed Sassani's penchant for dishonesty and the decadence that festered underneath their facade of bourgeois respectability. These negative perceptions of Sasso were further exacerbated by the allegations of graft and abuse of office that were being levied against Sassano officials. When the Twin Peaks incident hit the scene, a number of local politicians were being investigated by Italian authorities for the mismanagement of European development funds. The political intrigues of the community were well publicized in the media and lent the Twin Peaks affair even greater social significance.

In the local media, however, it was "Southerners" and foreign criminals who were held accountable for the Twin Peaks fiasco. An article entitled "*La calda estate del Twin Peaks*" (The Long, Hot Summer of Twin Peaks) represented these regional and international others as the forces responsible for infiltrating the peaceful, unsuspecting community of Sasso. According to a report from the province-wide newspaper *Il Centro*, Sasso had fallen victim to a band of mafiosi drug pushers from the South. The article accused these Southerners of tarnishing Sasso's reputation, specifically naming Campania as the region of the crime ring (*Il Centro* 1994, 2).

Despite the provincial press's bucolic depiction of rural life in the Abruzzo, stories of prostitution and illicit sex are not new to Sasso. One of the most persistent rumors that I heard during my fieldwork alleged the existence of a house of prostitution in the center of town; in these rumors, the brothel was run by the community's most respected women. Unlike the reports of the province-wide newspaper, which depict the forces of evil as external to Sasso, the local rumor mill suggests that Sasso itself is the source of sexual transgression.

Walking home one night, my friend Cristina spun out the story of Sasso's downtown brothel. According to her, the prostitution house was staffed by a clandestine group of Sassano "signore" (ladies) who, by day, posed as respectable housewives and mothers and, by night, sold their bodies for money. I asked Cristina to show me where the house was located, and she identified a reception hall downtown that was used for weddings and parties. The house of ill repute was conveniently situated next to one of the hotels in the piazza. When I would press Cristina for details she would say, "*Così dicono*" (That's what they say). Cristina was a walking broadside of entertaining stories about cheating husbands and women who lured men into their homes. These tales, however, were more like titillating references than full-blown narratives; schematic, they failed to stand up to scrutiny when I pressed her for information. On these occasions, Cristina and I would laugh at her penchant for exaggeration and the ludicrous vision of the townsfolk engaged in a bacchanalian frenzy.

While the rumors of the downtown brothel may be pure fiction, they are nonetheless remarkably telling. It is interesting to note that, in the town's gossip, people focused their criticisms on the women who allegedly worked as prostitutes, rather than on the men who allegedly employed them. Why does the rumor attack "respectable wives" and not "upstanding husbands"? In the case of Twin Peaks, why does the mainstream press search for regional others to blame?

In the response of older Sassano women to the Twin Peaks scandal, we see a direct critique of modernity. That a disco (a symbol of decadence) named Twin Peaks (an icon of American corruption even more reprehensible than *Beautiful*) really *was* a home to drugs and prostitution is seen to vindicate their criticism of modernity. The regional press, however, is committed to representing the Abruzzo as bucolic and pristine and, as a result, scapegoats Southerners and foreigners as the source of corruption.

Unlike the Twin Peaks scandals, the downtown brothel rumor was created by Sassani for Sassani. It reflects the inner doubt that they have about their town and modernity. On the surface, the rumor suggests, we Sassani appear to be upstanding citizens. Underneath it all, however, the criticisms that Roccaspinians and Bevilaquans hurl at us are true; our officials are corrupt and our most well-bred women are prostitutes. Further, it is respectable women of wealth (rather than those from the working class) who stray from the straight and narrow path – suggesting that the depravity of modernity comes from the affluence and political corruption of the bourgeoisie. Finally, it is important to see how these narratives reveal longstanding ideas about sexuality in Italian culture. In traditional Italy, it is women who are responsible for maintaining control over sexuality; men, it is believed, cannot control their desires and cannot be held accountable for transgressions like premarital sex, out-of-wedlock birth, or adultery. Thus, in the downtown brothel rumor, it is the wealthy and deceitful seductresses, not the men who patronized them, who are responsible for Sasso's moral decline. In modernity, the rumor suggests, even the most respectable women in the town have abdicated their role as sexual gatekeepers. Corruption is the result.

Twin Peaks illustrates the various pressures that bear down upon the citizens of Sasso: from the ongoing issues of female chastity to the confusion about modernizing gender roles, shame over local corruption, and class tensions in the context of a developing economy. But the Twin Peaks scandal was a short-lived moment in Sasso's history. In order to get a richer perspective on how gender, class, and modernity play themselves out in the town, we need to look at an element of local culture which is more ongoing and profound – the passeggiata. While the Twin Peaks scandal reveals Sassani's deep fear of modernity and changing sexual mores, it does not explore the ways in which people creatively engage with these cultural influences in their everyday life as the passeggiata does. By examining this rich sphere of expressive culture we can gain a better appreciation for ways in which Sassani actively experiment with and explore the notions of gender and modernity.

5

Seeing and Being Seen
in the Sassano Passeggiata

In chapters 3 and 4, I examined a broad array of cultural forms and tried to illustrate the social issues that concern the residents of Sasso. Interpreting *L'Istruttoria* or *Giochi Senza Frontiere, Milagros,* or the Ylenia affair, my discussion showed how Sassani use expressive culture to think about and debate the concept of modernity. Rather than looking at a variety of genres, this chapter explores just one expressive domain, the centerpiece of the town's social life, Sasso's beloved passeggiata.

While this chapter limits the number of genres under consideration, it simultaneously expands the analytic scope. Where the last two chapters examined the meanings of particular cultural forms, my analysis of the passeggiata, here, will look at both the meanings of the event and the expressive practices by which those meanings are established. Though folklorists have identified a wide range of features vital to the functioning of festivals and large-scale public display events (Falassi 1987; Stoeltje 1992; Manning 1992), the dynamics of seeing and being seen have largely been ignored by scholars in our field. Building upon ideas about the presentation of self and performance in the work of Erving Goffman (1959, 1961, 1967, 1972, 1983) and Richard Bauman (1977, 1983, 1989), this chapter describes in detail how, through the act of seeing, Sassani attach meaning to the clothing, posture, gait, gesture, and glances of others, and how their own presentation of those elements is oriented toward the fact of being seen. While the section does not provide a minute account of the movement of eyes and the swiveling of heads, it takes seeing seriously and treats visual perception as the primary way in which meaning is made in the passeggiata.

My concern for both social meanings and the expressive practices that establish them is consonant with the interests of the townsfolk; Sassani are committed to perfecting the skills of performance. More importantly, however, the passeggiata is a collective conversation about the meaning of modernity, and for Sassani the problems of modernity are bound up with issues of aesthetics.[1] To be modern is to display a refined, urban sensibility, and the different segments of Sassano society use the passeggiata to lay claim to this value in different ways. Middle-aged, professional women in Sasso declare themselves as modern by promenading in conservative designer tailleurs (French for "tailored suits"); young women flaunt the greater freedom their generation has attained by wearing the flamboyant fashions of Italy's major cities;[2] all participants seek to achieve *bella figura* and depict local identity as cosmopolitan and urbane. As I illustrate in chapter 6, Sassani recognize the price of progress but seek to transcend it by making modern life an aesthetic project. The passeggiata is the place where that project is learned, rehearsed, debated, and achieved.

In the first parts of this chapter, I will explore how participation in the passeggiata is informed by gender, age, and class, and I will discuss how the key concepts of *bella figura* and disinvoltura shape Sassano actions in this expressive sphere. Shifting from performance to reception, the second part examines the ideology of *bodily divination*, an interpretive framework Sassani use to make sense of the conduct of others. In the last part, I will discuss how the participants co-opt the notion of modernity in their expressive displays to physically and symbolically stake out a place for themselves in the piazza and the wider culture.

THE PLAYERS ON THE STAGE

Sassani view the passeggiata as a performance. Unlike a presentation of an epic or a folk song, however, the roles of spectator and performer in the promenade are not immediately evident to the outside observer. We can begin our discussion by exploring the complex ways in which these roles are assigned in the piazza. At a basic level, participants can frame their actions as more or less performative by their choice of clothing and the location of their strolling on the street. Maximally performative participants dress to the nines and stroll down the center of the street, while those who desire less public attention walk along the side of *il corso*. It is the strollers "heightened

Figure 27   Widows viewing the passeggiata from their terrace (video still from
the author's field tapes)

awareness toward their own acts of expression" that keys the audience to watch with greater intensity and "interpret what they say [or
do] in some special sense" (Bauman 1977, 9). Those who choose to
watch the proceedings, rather than perform, are largely segregated
by gender, with the men viewing the event from the sidewalk bars
and the older women and widows observing from terraces and
stoops (figures 27–9).

The expressive density of the passeggiata makes it difficult, at
times, to pick out the performers from the nonperformers. In fact,
these two categories exist on a smooth continuum in the passeggiata.
At one end of the spectrum are the men who mill about the sidewalk
bars and the garden; they are clearly not on display. The teenage boys
who gather on the street corner revving up the motors of their Vespa
mopeds are on the boundary between performer and spectator. Any
strollers, particularly female strollers, in the center of the street are
in full performance, and participants frequently shift between these
categories. For example, when a team of avid walkers leave the
center of the street to buy ice-cream, they gear down into a less
performative mode; nevertheless, because they are grouped together
and wearing their finest attire, their behavior is still marginally performative. And, while those observing from the bars and porches are
not considered to be promenading, to even appear in the piazza

Figure 28   Older men viewing the passeggiata from the garden, with statue of the Madonna in the background (video still from the author's field tapes)

Figure 29   Older men viewing the passeggiata from a sidewalk café (video still from the author's field tapes)

between five thirty and eight is to submit oneself to a sophisticated aesthetic of public scrutiny.

While almost everyone in the town participates in the promenade, the responsibilities for performance vary by gender, age, and class. For example, there is a tacit understanding in Sasso that women are most responsible for the performances that occur in the piazza. As the leading figures in this theatrical display, they are seen to have a social obligation to entertain the crowd with their feminine charms and pleasing appearance. Although men, too, contribute their special brand of expressivity, there is a greater burden on women to *mettersi in mostra* (put oneself on display). The amount of time that women spend primping and preening before the passeggiata not only testifies to Sassani's concern with appearance and demeanor, it also speaks to the gender divisions that exist in this sphere. While, in general, attention is only paid to men if they look exceptionally good or bad, the female strollers are always on display – even if they are not in full performance mode. The higher standards to which females are held pressure them to look their best in the piazza. As we've seen in chapter 1, some Sassano women strongly resented these cultural attitudes; for others, the expectation to pay attention to the details of dress and to perform in public was perceived as an aesthetic opportunity rather than a hardship.[3]

It is in the passeggiata that young women receive their first lessons in womanhood. Here, they become adept at manipulating the secret codes of gender-specific body language and learn the rules of decorous conduct. As the training ground of gender roles par excellence, the passeggiata is where Sassano girls are socialized to think of themselves as objects of vision, desire, and admiration – a sight to be consumed. Through the friendly scolding of older women and the examples set by others, girls are schooled in the corporeal mastery of *bella figura*.

The acquisition of gendered skills of social interaction is closely related to a second function of the event, that of a marriage market. To many in Sasso, especially the older generation, the passeggiata is considered a respectable place for the proper young woman to find a husband. While the event was once the primary site for socially sanctioned courting, this status has decreased somewhat. Dating practices and courtship rituals have become less formal and proscriptive in Sasso, and single men and women can more freely interact in public settings. Teenage boys and girls will rendezvous in couples on the passeggiata or at their favorite downtown establishments and are free to casually socialize in large groups, with or without their parents' knowledge. Among an older set, single adults with cars and financial means who wish to avoid the prying eyes of the community may avoid the piazza and opt to date in nearby urban centers like Vasto or Pescara. Those who are engaged or are in long-term relationships, however, can often be seen walking together on Corso Vittorio Emanuele. The passeggiata of the Easter holidays, patron-Saint feast days or locally organized community events in Sasso attract visitors from the outside, and, on these occasions, paesani and friends enjoy long evening strolls and catch up on news, while strangers from the neighboring villages mingle with the townsfolk. These are opportune moments for unmarried individuals to meet prospective mates.

Even though the passeggiata is predicated on the participation of women, there are men in the community who lament the feminine presence in this space. In interviews and everyday conversations, Sassano men often criticized what they considered to be the female penchant for public display and spoke condescendingly about *"la vanità e il narcisismo delle donne"* (the vanity and narcissism of women). A few men with whom I spoke, however, sympathized with women's enthusiasm for the passeggiata. As I suggested in the previous chapter, the public sphere has traditionally been associated with men, and even today there are few culturally sanctioned public spaces beyond the passeggiata where women can congregate and socialize. As Antonio Grafa, a leftist political dissenter told me, *"Non c'è niente da fare qui per le donne; non ci sono associazioni o centri di ritrovo"* (There is nothing here for women to do; there are no associations or gathering places).

Whether they seek a husband, a boyfriend, or just a culturally acceptable place for public sociability, young women are the most noticeable participants of the Sassano passeggiata. Indeed these passeggiata regulars amuse the local townsfolk with their lively antics and provocative ways. Defiant or respectful, loud or quiet, colorful or understated, as a group these teenage women elicited a great deal of attention from onlookers. Even small gestures or acts of studied indifference could prompt participants to look their way. In fact their youthful displays of female exuberance were frequently admired by the old-timers who liked to sit on the benches by the *Madonnina*. One day when I asked the older men with their canes and jaunty hats what it is that they were looking at exactly, they smiled and replied, *"ma guardiamo queste belle ragazze nel fiore della gioventù"* (but we are looking at these beautiful girls who are in the flower of their youth). As we will see below, the sometimes boisterous performances of female sexuality – and the scandalized responses of the older women in the community – have become a standard feature of the event.

If young women are the leading figures in the passeggiata, widows and senior citizens are the supporting cast members. Widows are relegated to the role of spectator and wear distinctive cultural markers to convey their nonperforming status. With their traditional lutto, they typically enjoy the affair from their stoops or terrace balconies. Avid audience members, they often sit together in semi-circles performing needlework, chatting, and gossiping about the day's news while they watch and comment upon passersby. As we saw in chapter 1, these women are the guardians of traditional gender roles in Sasso; they are expected to lead modest, exemplary lives and are strongly discouraged from participating in the mainstream of the town's social life. As such, they do not perform in the passeggiata, though their spectating is a crucial feature of the event. Wearing frumpy headscarves or tattered jackets, senior citizens of both sexes are another group of spectators. Because of their age, they are no longer seen as competitors for jobs, spouses, or political favors; as a result, they appear in informal clothing that younger people – with much more to lose – would never consider wearing.[4]

Though class is no longer a barrier to passeggiata performance, it continues to influence the meanings that participation in the event has for Sassani. The old feudal taboos that forbade people of different social rankings to mix are still alive in Sassano memory and serve as a wedge between groups. Despite the changing social relations brought about by modernity, some Sassani continue to equate the passeggiata with the upper echelons of Italian society. However, as we have seen in chapter 1, what used to be the exclusive domain of the rich is now available to the rising Sassano middle class, who only a few decades ago had neither the means nor the permission to enter this sphere. My experiences with Paola, a middle-aged, working-class woman will suggest some of these dynamics.

No matter how many times I asked her, Paola repeatedly declined my invitations to go on the promenade. On our occasional walks together, Paola routinely avoided Corso Vittorio Emanuele and preferred instead to take leisurely strolls on the newly built stretch of road near the costa delle zitelle (the cliff of the old maids). When I asked her why she avoided walking on Sasso's thoroughfare, Paola gave me a variety of reasons and rationales. The first time I asked her to join me, she declined by saying that she was not suitably dressed. On another occasion, she told me that she didn't want her husband to see her walking in the piazza before supper when she should be at home preparing the evening meal. While Paola always steered clear of Sasso's main streets during the peak hours of the passeggiata, she did treat herself to late afternoon walks in the cemetery and quick jaunts through the side streets. Here, the rules of etiquette and the judgmental eyes of the community were not quite as oppressive.

These cultural restrictions, however, don't fully explain Paola's complex feelings about the passeggiata, and her discomfort hid more profound reasons for avoiding Sasso's favorite pastime. During my fieldwork, Paola and I spent a great deal of time with each other. As she lived nearby and was a friend of my family, we spoke or shared a meal almost every day. Over the course of many conversations and daily interactions, I discovered that her reluctance to participate in the passeggiata stemmed from her feelings of being excluded from the mainstream of Sassano life. As I suggested in chapter 1, the passeggiata is often represented as an icon of the greater social equality brought about by modern liberal democracy. With her husband's left politics and her modest contadino background, Paola did not see the event in this way; for her, the promenade's promise of upward mobility was a cruel reminder of her own lack of social advancement. She and her family had suffered greatly under the decades of Democratic Christian rule in Sasso. Her husband's vocal opposition to the political establishment had stigmatized the family and severely compromised their role in the community. After numerous failed attempts to find employment, her son finally moved to Germany. Paola herself was wrongfully dismissed from her factory job by company men who sought to curry favor with local officials. These life experience have circumscribed Paola's participation in the passeggiata and soured its display of bourgeois cosmopolitanism and capitalist consumption.

BELLA FIGURA **AND DISINVOLTURA**

Two underlying concepts are crucial for any understanding of the passeggiata: *bella figura* and disinvoltura. This section explores these concepts and shows how they are variously enacted by the concrete practices of "being seen" (i.e., performance) in the promenade.

In Sasso the desire to *fare bella figura* is brought into being every time Sassani perform their ritual vasche. As we have seen in chapter 1, Sassani make a metaphorical correspondence between the piazza and the human form: the area behind the church being the head and the far end of Corso Vittorio Emanuele being the feet. Tracing out the contours of this figure with their elegant laps, they physically and symbolically make beautiful the body social. Not merely the aesthetic standard for the passeggiata, the notion of *bella figura* is a general principle of etiquette and taste for all spheres of social life in Sasso.

For example, at a Sassano wedding it is customary to bring an envelope with money. In the local ideology of gift exchange, such presents are considered a "prestito" (loan), which is reciprocated by giving similar amounts to other newlyweds in the future. Failing to live up to these rules of reciprocity, a guest runs the risk of losing face or *fare una brutta figura* (literally, to make a bad face or to make bad impression). A social gaff of great stupidity is usually referred to as *una figuraccia* (literally, a big ugly face or a terrible impression). With their penchant for exaggeration and their sensitivity to social inappropriateness, Sassano teenagers are particularly fond of the expression "*Che figuraccia!*" (literally, what a big ugly face or what a terrible impression) emphasizing the "*Che*" to dramatize the level of embarrassment.[5]

In Sasso, the skillful execution of *bella figura* is nowhere more important than in the promenade; here, the art of public display is given full reign. *Bella figura* is largely measured in terms of demeanor and presentational style. Attire, grooming, posture, physical grace, manners, and conversational skills are carefully monitored and judged. While expensive clothing is valued, one need not be wealthy to cut a fine figure. It is better to walk with a smooth gait and wear a pleasing combination of simple clothes than to slouch about in designer fashions or wear expensive garments that are ill-fitting or poorly coordinated. Recognition is another key part of the passeggiata, and failure to greet and acknowledge others is a serious offense. In Sassani's eyes, those who are unable to meet the standards of politeness and sociability reveal their lack of social refinement and character.

Fare bella figura is particularly important because the passeggiata is the main place in which reputations are won or lost. For young men and women, one's clothing, gait, and demeanor mark one as respectable or ill mannered, marriageable or poorly suited for matrimony. Further, the ability to *fare bella figura* helps to establish one's integrity and social standing within the community. Passeggiata performances mark a person as respectable, hardworking, and trustworthy, or, alternatively, as lazy, slovenly, or uncouth. The maintenance of one's public persona is crucial in a small society where raccomandazioni are the key to jobs and political benefits. Repeated acts of *brutta figura* degrade one's reputation, which in turn can have serious consequences for one's economic well being.

The most talented performers possess what the Italians call disinvoltura. Ideally, a passeggiata performer should have a spontaneous and unselfconscious personal style. The term "disinvoltura" can be used interchangeably with "sprezzatura," and the two have their roots

Figure 30   The distracted walker (video still from the author's field tapes)

in the aesthetics of courtly behavior of early modern Italy. In *The Book of the Courtier*, Baldessare Castiglione's guide to etiquette for the elite palaces of the sixteenth century, the great arbiter of style and manners explains that proper behavior "springs chiefly from sprezzatura, an air of perfect naturalness acquired through discipline" (Castiglione 1976 [1528]). While few Sassani have read Castiglione, most are aware of the passeggiata's historical association with the gentry and the aesthetic of effortless style. Paola's experiences not withstanding, many Sassani feel that it is the achievement of modernity to have opened up the quest for disinvoltura to all segments of society.

We can gain richer insights into these issues by exploring how the guiding concept of disinvoltura informs the concrete practices of "being seen" (i.e., performance) in the piazza. Significantly, disinvoltura is not achieved by marking social distinctions, but politely recognizing others. To be disinvolto, performers must acknowledge that they are performing and that others are paying attention to the performance, without drawing undue attention to either fact. The concept is best illustrated by a negative example. On one evening, a woman in her twenties whom I shall call the "distracted walker" promenades down the center of the street in a fine tailored suit of light beige; her hands are clasped in front of her in a gesture meant to evoke demure femininity (figure 30). As she walks along, however, she constantly turns her head to the left and right as if searching for a person in the crowd. She makes no effort to glance discretely or conceal her boredom with the event. Completely disengaged, she is, for all intents and purposes, a walking suit.

Though her dress is impeccable, she fails to achieve disinvoltura. As one looks at her, her clothes and location in the street frame her behavior as a performance and call for the other participants' attention. Her unconcealed distraction, however, tells the audience that we are not appearing in her experience. I videotaped a large number of strollers in the promenade, and all of the people with whom I did feedback interviews criticized this walker's absent-minded display and her failure to meet the gazes of oncoming strollers. Her clasped hands clashed with her bored facial expressions, the interviewees said.

She could improve her performance in one of two ways. If she walked on the side of the street or the sidewalk she would no longer attract the critical attention of others and would be free to search for her friend. In so doing, she would not achieve disinvoltura – this term is usually reserved for those in full performance mode – but neither would she *fare una brutta figura* and draw the opprobrium of the crowd. If she wishes to stay in the center of the street, she must keep her head forward, gracefully acknowledge the attention her performance prompts, and glance about for her friend with greater subtlety. But calling out for the attention of all present and clearly disattending to the event, this stroller cannot achieve disinvoltura, no matter how fine her tailored suit or how well coiffured her hair. Independent of her distraction, or even because of it, this woman's dress would almost certainty be considered stylish by onlookers in an American cultural context. But in an event dominated by an aesthetic of disinvoltura, such a performance was seen as a complete failure.[6]

To successfully achieve disinvoltura, participants must background the artifice of their actions. Dressing and grooming themselves, all strollers must actively prepare for the passeggiata, and, during the event, all are aware that they are being observed. The difficulty for the actor, therefore, lies in looking natural and unaffected while at the same time abiding by the complex rules of etiquette and decorum. A related paradox is found in one's metacommunicative signaling of one's self-awareness in the event. To be disinvolto, one must acknowledge other's awareness appropriately – indicating that one is the object of pubic attention without pompously strutting like an actor on a stage. Too much self-consciousness, and you are precious; too little, and you have pretensions of naïveté.

If the "distracted walker" illustrates disinvoltura through negative example, the displays of Rosa Di Roma, a stroller with a total disregard

Figure 31   Rosa Di Roma (video still from the author's field tapes)

for the concept, are more complex (figure 31). Examining the responses of the townsfolk to her performance can illustrate the varying ways in which Sassani apply this aesthetic principle in the passeggiata.

A popular woman in her early twenties, Rosa Di Roma is well known throughout the town for her unconventional clothing and style. While she sometimes wears short skirts, her passeggiata performances are not especially sexualized, and she is best known in the piazza for her heavy, thick-soled Jean-Paul Gauthier shoes and the sharp contrast of her naturally pale complexion with her raven-dyed hair and black, Cher-inspired eyeliner. A conventional top, jacket, and haircut round out her look.

Such elements of style make a statement in themselves; while the shoes, eyeliner, and hair color reference the contemporary and assertive fashions of Rome or Milan, her unexceptional clothing downplays the significance of style, suggesting a cooler attitude to the event and the high value the town places upon it. But clothing never appears in the passeggiata by itself, and the metacommunicative signals that accompany the performance color and transform the overall aesthetic effect generated by Rosa's strolling. An infrequent participant in the passeggiata, Rosa does not achieve disinvoltura in the conventional sense. While she fails to acknowledge the passersby in the traditional manner, she is not as oblivious to her surroundings as the "distracted walker" was to hers; instead, her gaze registers the fact that others are watching but communicates neither anxious concern for the others' reactions nor haughty disdain for their attention. Her reactions to the others' performance is equally neutral, betraying neither pleasure nor disgust. In sum, Rosa is indifferent to the attention and the performance of others.

The interpretations of her multifaceted display vary. In conversations, several traditional Sassani said that they see Rosa as "*una ragazza ribelle*" (a rebellious young woman). While designer clothes are popular on the passeggiata, Chanel suits and tailored outfits are the looks that appeal to the more conservative townsfolk. Though her heavy shoes and retro-sixties eyeliner may reference the fashionable styles of Italy's major cities, Rosa's detractors see her nonchalant demeanor and unpresupposing top and skirt as a criticism of their widely held belief in the cosmopolitan values of elegance and refinement. Her short skirt and light-black nylon stockings blantantly challenge Sassano notions of female respectability. On two separate occasions spectators quipped, "*È troppo esagerata, sembra un pagliaccio*" (She is too exaggerated, she looks like a clown) and "*Non è un abbigliamento adatto per la passeggiata*" (This dress is not suitable for the passeggiata). For mainstream segments of the population, Rosa's unorthodox appearance implies a symbolic refusal to comply with community standards of beauty and sophestication. To say, however, that Rosa doesn't give a damn altogether about public approval is also not entirely accurate, because her use of streetstyles in the event is restrained – embracing heavy lipstick and eyeliner but avoiding piercings and tattoos, for example. To her detractors, Rosa's clothing was less problematic than her style of interaction, specifically her failure to recognize the glances of others and show them the proper deference. In the feedback interviews, those who were critical of Rosa directed their primary attacks at her bored demeanor and lack of engagement with others in the event.

Some Sassani, however, approve of Rosa's display. While these residents see her shoes, eyeliner, and hair as a stylish, daring statement, such objects are made meaningful by her comportment and demeanor. Rosa's supporters see her indifferent gaze in the context of her only occasional participation in the event and of her prosaic top and skirt. As a result, they interpret her nonchalant glance – not as an affectation of boredom – but as a reflection of genuine indifference. From this perspective, Rosa is experienced as her own person, a cosmopolitan figure who enjoys the pleasures of dressing up (the shoes, the eyeliner, and so forth) but is neither mired in the time-consuming rituals of shopping and pre-passeggiata preparation, nor impressed by the displays of the other townsfolk. However, if Rosa completely ignored the presence of others or wore aggressively cheap or disheveled clothing, she would almost certainly loose these supporters and be interpreted as nothing more than obnoxious poseur. But her combination of stylish and common clothing and the (perceived) effortlessness of her indifference serve as metacommunicative signals of a genuinely partial engagement with the event. Such signals inform the overall aesthetic effect of her performance, producing a sense of stylishness that resists the more restrictive options of Chanel-suit respectability and high-fashion coquetry that, we shall see, are common in the passeggiata.

This sense of style has affinities with the traditional notion of disinvoltura. To be disinvolto, however, is to display a comfort with one's place in the town and, by implication, to endorse community values; like the successful courtier, a person who is disinvolto is a solid citizen as well as a stylish one. Rosa's performance implies a subtle disdain for the town, and, as such, her performance would not be seen as an example of disinvoltura, even by her supporters. Such fine points of interpretation can be read in many ways, and it was for this reason that Rosa was frequently the topic of debate in the Sassano passeggiata.

BODILY DIVINATION

Though the concepts of *bella figura* and disinvoltura inform interpretation as well as action, they are primarily understood as guides to correct conduct. Conversely, the principle of *bodily divination*[7] is primarily an interpretive framework, a set of ideas that inform the practices of seeing in the passeggiata. While the act of reading another's body language is a universal human activity, each culture achieves these interpretations by reference to local ideas about the body, the character, and the self.

In Sasso, such interpretations are often predicated on the belief that each individual has an immutable essence, a moral nature that is both stable and innate. Unearthing this essence, however, is not an easy task. On the one hand, Sassani see the body as an oracle of the human soul; on the other hand, Sassani recognize that actors chronically manipulate the images they project. Constantly aware of the tension between these ideas, Sassani seek to pierce the veil of the other's impression management (Goffman 1959) and glimpse the ethical core of the person they believe lurks within. This faith in a stable moral character obscured by artifice but ultimately discoverable through skillful observation forms an ideology of interpretation I will refer to as bodily divination. In piecing together clues, hunches, and information gleaned from everyday encounters, Sassani bring different sensibilities and rhetorical strategies to bear upon the problem of discerning the essence of the other.

Bodily divination in Sasso involves attention to a wide variety of clues including, but not limited to, dress, comportment, demeanor, gesture, proxemics, and posture. But how are we to understand this varied assortment of signs and reconcile them with the primacy of the body? Erving Goffman once observed that the "body exudes expressions" (1969, 5). This is true, but when operationalizing this notion in fieldwork, the idea of the body immediately becomes problematic. The body exudes expression, but, to understand embodied social practices in ethnographic research, we must recognize that it does so through a number of dimensions and linkages.

For example, costume is a dimension of the body. While the suit that one wears is obviously not a part of one's body, it is absurd to speak of clothing without also discussing the body to which that clothing is literally tailored. Deportment is another dimension of bodily practice; by deportment I mean the various postures in which the arms, neck, back, and hands are held. In the abstract, the range of bodily deportment is only constrained by the actor's kinesic wit. In the concrete, however, all but the most skilled dancer find deportment to be distinct from simple volitional activity. For most of us, deportment, like breathing, is the meeting place of the body as a predetermined biological mechanism and the body as a medium of intentional activity. It is the kinetic ground from which more directly volitional bodily practices emerge. And, while speech and gesture exist at the far end of the dialectic of the body as object and the body-subject, contemporary research by writers as different as George Lakoff (1987) and Maurice Merleau-Ponty (1981) suggests that the two can never be divorced. Independent of these academic debates, the Sassani's interpretation of others in the piazza entwines costume, deportment, gesture, and the body in an inextricable whole, and it is this ensemble that is understood as the symptom of an individual's underlying character. Never fully controlled, but always potentially open to manipulation, the expressions of the body are dynamic and interactive. It is the pre-reflexive body that Sassani seek as an oracle of character.

In the bustling interpretive marketplace of the passeggiata, deportment is one of the most important indicators of internal qualities. Erect posture, for example, is often equated with feminine virtue and self-possession. Likewise, moderately paced strolling and a front-oriented gaze is viewed as an extension of the ideal female temperament. (The distracted walker is a negative example of this bodily comportment.) While styles of walking are sometimes seen to express a person's status in the society, they are more often interpreted as reflections of character. In this context, a pleasing countenance not only reveals an affable personality but an interior goodness that transcends manners. While the elegantly dressed woman can, by virtue of her appearance and demeanor, radiate social refinement, her deportment will be seen as the sign of trustworthiness. As I describe in chapter 1, to be *"retto e corretto"* (literally, upright and correct) in Sasso is to be an upstanding, praiseworthy person, one whose physical bearing displays moral rectitude (figures 18–19).

It is through the process of video feedback interviews that I came to discover the Sassano ideology of bodily divination. This technique helped to reveal to what spectators paid attention in the piazza. In the initial stages of the research, almost everyone who participated in the feedback interviews watched the videotapes of Sasso with curiosity and amusement. While some people remarked at how beautiful the town looked, others made disparaging comments about their fellow townsfolk's penchant for fanatical self-display. In the first five minutes of video-viewing, Sassani usually tried to recognize people in the crowd, identifying them by their clan names and relationships to others in the community. In the midst of the banter, humorous quips, and sarcasm, my informants began to slowly impute specific meanings to the participants' behavior. More than off-the-cuff remarks about particular styles of presentation, these comments were snapshot assessments of character. Through a series of rapid mental observations, informants took certain features to be signs of intrinsic qualities. At this point in my research it became clear that the act of looking was more than an idle pastime, but a complex cultural practice for gauging the true essence of an other.

A case in point from the interviews is the interpretations of a woman I will call the "haughty walker." The individual received sharp criticism for her behavior in the passeggiata from all of the Sassani who viewed the tapes. Parading down the center of the street in a skirt, sweater, blazer, and pumps, her proud, mechanical gait marked her walking as a very self-conscious performance. At the same time, however, she conspicuously failed to make eye contact or greet passersby, a fact that the interviewees interpreted as active and ostentatious disattention. As a result, her walk displayed contradictory messages – "I am performing, pay attention," and "I don't see you, I am alone on *il corso*." This metacommunicative dissonance was experienced as rudeness. More importantly, the Sassani who viewed the tape did not see her erect posture as a sign of virtue. Stiff and controlled, her back posture was interpreted as self-conscious artifice, rather than a natural reflection of inner uprightness. Maria, a life-long Sassana, described the haughty walker's gait as ridiculously forced and indicative of arrogance. "Look at her *tutta impostata* [dialect for 'all stiff and conceited']. She is arrogant and superior." Tiziana, another interviewee, interpreted the same over-controlled body language in terms of her knowledge of the woman's past: "She [the 'haughty walker'] is nothing more than a stupid woman who has made money because of the Democratic Christians. Her grand-mother was a pitzante [dialect for 'a poor devil'] who only had one dress to wear. Now she walks impostata and with her nose in the air."

In the passeggiata itself, such character assessments are an almost constant accompaniment to the participants' experience, and often only the slightest gesture or facial expression is needed to evoke such a response. In the piazza one night, for example, I overheard a young Sassano woman say, "Look at his [a male stroller's] eyes; he is so avaristic and greedy." While this remark was but a fleeting observa-tion in the running commentary that makes up the passeggiata, it points to a crucial aspect of the event. Fast-moving gestures and furtive glances are the stuff of which the promenade is made, and, intentionally or not, individuals in this milieu continuously evoke moods, meanings, and reactions through their behavior. This almost constant flow of character judgements can hold a range of positions in the participant's experience: from the background to the fore-ground of attention, from internal ruminations to isolated remarks to extended debates about the character of others.

Agreed upon or contested, bodily divination is sometimes repre-sented as a kind of magic or an inspired guess. On some occasions a particularly effective interpretation of character may be represented as a moment of lucidity, a flash of second sight otherwise reserved for saints or those with paranormal powers. Seen in this light, bodily divination takes on an almost mystical quality, and the connections between contemporary interpretative practices and longstanding tra-ditions in Italian esoteric thought is a provocative one. Discussing ideas about the relationship between the face and the soul in medieval Italy, Patrizia Magli describes a belief in a "cosmic system of corre-spondence" that highlights the relationship between "microcosm and macrocosm" (1989, 367). In this cultural "taxonomy of [quasi-]perma-nent moral characteristics," as Magli puts it, "the world appears in a symptomatic way, wherein things are signs of other things" (Magli 1989, 103). As with tarot card reading or other forms of augury, bodily divination is the search for insight into a more fundamental reality. If, in the tarot, "The Lightning-Struck Tower" card represents conflict or unforeseen catastrophe and "The Four of Wands" points to the coming of romance, harmony, prosperity, and peace (Gray 1960), in Sassano society it is the physical characteristics of human beings and of the body in performance that gives diviners entry into hidden dimensions. Hence, in Sassani's ideology of bodily divination, thin lips may correspond to greed, and a careless appearance can be seen as a manifestation of a disorderly inner temperament. Similarly, good or bad posture (and too much or too little attention to posture) can be equally interpreted as a telling sign of another's true nature. Here, deportment can betray character, despite the actor's most studious efforts to control their presentation of self.

As we have seen, the practice of bodily divination is dependent on the underlying assumption that character is a timeless essence or soul discernable through outward manifestations. When applied to local history, gossip, and kinship ties, this assumption results in an interpretative framework that we might call the mystical analysis of history. Using this framework, Sassani search the stories of a person's family to reveal the essence of the other, and the approach is best summed up in the familiar Sassano proverb, "*Dimmi di chi sei la figlia e ti dirò chi sei*" (Tell me of whom you are the daughter, and I shall tell you who you are"). Understood in this way, the soul is not merely a timeless essence, unique to the individual, but an inherited essence whose nature is revealed in the deeds of one's predecessors. Here, acts of loyalty or betrayal, generosity or penury in the previous generation of one's family function like the thin lips or wandering eyes of the passeggiata performer, revealing to the adept observer the true nature of the person in question. It is important to emphasize that the twin frameworks of bodily divination and the mystical interpretation of history are not the only tools that Sassani use to understand the nature of others. The townsfolk recognize, of course, that a good person can come from a family with a bad reputation, that generous people can have close-set eyes, and that character can operate as a disposition to act rather than a fixed essence. Nevertheless these quasi-occult interpretative frameworks are part of Sassano culture, and divinatory practices such as these are two key devices in the Sassano toolkit.

While character judgement may be interpreted as mystical insight, Sassani often view bodily divination as a battle of cunning and will. In fact, the conflict between the stroller's presentation of self and the interpreter's capacity for penetrating observation provides the passeggiata with one of its central tensions. Paradoxically the very emphasis on appearance and polite decorum in the piazza leads Sassani to speculate about the deception that lies beneath the patina of social niceties. Participants frequently expressed the belief that the town's pretension to civiltà is a sham and that the strollers' displays of *bella figura* and disinvoltura are nothing but a game of trickery. The social observer, therefore, is given the task of probing the deeper meanings that underlie bodily expressions by carefully studying and analyzing the interactions that take place in the piazza.

One evening, for example, I strolled the piazza with Cristina, a Sassano native in her early twenties. In the middle of one of our vasche, we passed a man named Gianfranco coming along in the opposite direction. A middle-aged teacher at the local high school, Gianfranco wore brown, crepe-soled shoes, loose fitting, beige corduroy pants, a navy-blue, button-down shirt, and a bulky pullover sweater. While his clothes were not particularly distinctive, his comportment marked him as an academic – or a man with academic pretensions. He strolled *il corso* with a measured gate. Part of the time, his gaze was directed toward the ground, like a man lost in thought. The rest of the time, his eyes seemed to pick out individual objects in the piazza and subject them to a slow, thoughtful scrutiny; this gazing technique suggested a careful engagement with specific objects in the environment, like that of a botanist strolling the forest. Gianfranco's gazing techniques were accompanied by an intermittent rubbing of the chin, and often his hands were clasped behind his back in a gesture associated with older men.

When Gianfranco had passed out of earshot, Cristina said, "*Guardalo!*" (Look at him!) and expressed disgust at what she interpreted as Gianfranco's disingenuous style. No one could be as thoughtfully attentive and absent-mindedly reflective as his gaze suggested he was. His measured pace and self-conscious manual gestures were affectations, not natural habits, and his performance was contrived, an inauthentic display of scholarly wisdom. Cristina's interpretation was presented as a cunning penetration of Gianfranco's facade. Revealing his deportment to be a product of artifice rather than a natural expression of personal style, Cristina believed that she gained a key insight into Gianfranco's character. It is important to note that Cristina had crossed swords with Gianfranco in the past, and there is little doubt that her animosity toward him contributed to her critical interpretation of his comportment. Nevertheless, Cristina represented her readings as a penetrating vision into Gianfranco's character. Whether one takes Cristina's assertions at face value or questions the motives behind her remarks, one thing is certain: she is using the rhetoric of bodily divination to justify her vision of

Gianfranco's passeggiata performance. In this context, bodily divination is as much a form of discourse invoked to legitimate beliefs and attitudes as it is a system of ideas for understanding the character of others.

Perhaps the most important feature of character in the passeggiata is trustworthiness. Strolling the piazza, the most common comments are *"È una brava persona"* (What a good and honest person) or *"È una cattiva persona"* (What a mean, dishonest person). Here, I do not mean to suggest that bodily divination is used as a device for short-term, instrumental spying. A young Sassano man seeking a promotion at work will not tail his boss in pursuit of signs of dishonesty or dependability. On the contrary, bodily divination operates more as a constant accompaniment to the other events in the piazza. Sassani are concerned with seeking insight into the character of others, and any piece of knowledge that is obtained may be useful at some future point. Sassani have always felt that such social skills are crucial for staying afloat in the local society, and during my research the emphasis on trustworthiness was made even greater by the tangentopoli scandals and the prominant role that Sasso played in this public crisis of character.

If posture, clothing, and so forth are seen as indicators of inner nature, passeggiata participants can focus on either half of this equation. Focusing on bodily display rather than the character it betrays, the passeggiata participant's experience is primarily aesthetic. Focusing on the character who is allegedly indicated by performance rather than the performance itself, the participant's experience is consumed with character judgments and social assessments. But because bodily performance and character are so tightly linked in the local ideology, because in the local view performance and character are two sides of the same coin, it is rarely the case that either term is completely absent from the participant's experience. Focusing on the unattractive asymmetry of a poorly tucked shirt or a fluid, pleasing gait, the passeggiata participant has a distant awareness that this aesthetic faux pas or triumph maybe seen as reflecting character – if only because of the fact that the person is failing, or succeeding, to put the best foot forward. Searching another's face for trustworthiness or gauging another's gait for signs of stiffness, aesthetic qualities are not absent from the interpretation but serve as the means to those interpretative ends. In the local ideology beautiful performance and good character may occupy a number of complicated positions relative to one another, but they are seldom seen as disconnected.

The expressive poles of passeggiata performance can be emphasized with varying degrees of intensity. On a mundane level, effective aesthetic display facilitates casual sociability, while ineffective displays lead to boredom. However, when performers truly "hit their stride" in the promenade, they become attuned to their environment and enter into what I call the passeggiata zone. When one is in this zone, the rich play of sights, sounds, and pleasures all work to produce an intense gestalt of sensual feeling. Here, the sense modalities are engaged to full capacity and the strollers become hyperaware of their surroundings and their physical bodies. The exhilarating sensation of movement and aesthetic gratification is perhaps akin to the pleasure that some North Americans occasionally experience while driving and listening to music. During these special moments, the world seems to reveal itself as an object of unique beauty and meaning. Here, everyday life seems to be imbued with sharp sensual clarity and subjects become tremendously receptive to the natural and social universe.

Entrance into the passeggiata zone brings about a sense of enhanced corporeality. Here, the undisciplined array of arms, limbs, and surfaces are transformed into a smoothly coordinated ensemble of strolling bodies. During these intermittent periods of close proximity, communal solidarity, and expanded sensorial perception, bodily divination is backgrounded and the individual can indeed feel part of a larger whole – literally, a cell in the body politic. One is cognizant of one's body and also aware of an intense co-presence with the people who occupy the same social space. The self is experienced as at once distinct, yet inextricable, from others. Unlike the ecstatic states associated with meditative trances, the achievement of the passeggiata zone is not the main goal of the Sassano promenade, and such "flow experiences" (Csikszentmihalyi [1975] 2000) only occur occasionally. And unlike the communitas associated with the liminal phase of rites of passage (Turner 1969), the passeggiata zone does not transform social identity.

THE STAKING OF PLACE

Bella figura, disinvoltura, and bodily divination are the conceptual and aesthetic resources that inform the creation and interpretation of passeggiata performance. The rest of this chapter shifts focus, moving from the guiding concepts that enable performance to the rich meanings that those performances evoke and the social uses to which they are put. Some of these topics have already been introduced. Vying for position in the marriage market, maintaining their reputation through displays of respectability, divining the character of others, or providing themselves with entertainment and pleasure, Sassani use the passeggiata to achieve a wide variety of social goals. In this section, I will show how the townsfolk use passeggiata performance to stake a place for themselves in the community and create a representation – a kind of kinetic sculpture – of Sassano society. In the last section, I will build on this discussion and show how this collective representation of local identity serves as a forum for discussing the meaning of modernity.

It is not hard to understand how the ethnographer would interpret the passeggiata as a kind of kinetic sculpture of village society. Standing on a balcony with video camera in hand, I take in the event as a whole and see an image of local social life; power relations, generational conflicts, gender roles, and sociability all play themselves out before the social scientist's gaze. But to say that the passeggiata appears to an ethnographer as a image of Sassano society is a much weaker statement than the one I wish to make. I contend and will show how Sassani themselves see the passeggiata as a representation of the town and how their performances contribute to this improvisatory social theater.

This, too, may be understood in a straightforward sense. Sassani see an empty piazza as an image of rural boredom and a bustling piazza as a sign of their village's vitality and modernity. Townsfolk often speak of the cultural imperative to make *lo struscio* (literally, the big rub). The term refers to any kind of pleasant and flowing social interaction and the sense of warmth and sociability that such experiences engender. In numerous interviews, Sassani depicted this pursuit as both a biological need and social responsibility. The passeggiata is the site of *lo struscio* in Sasso. It invites citizens from all backgrounds to leisurely congregate in the public square and participate in the civilizing practice of artful conversation. During ferragosto these displays of local identity are placed within broader contexts. This period in August is peak vacation time throughout Italy; those from other parts of the country come to Sasso to enjoy the cool mountain air and nearby beach resorts, while Sasso's substantial outmigrant population returns to visit relatives and reconnect with their home. While the history of migration and remigration is never far from Sassano discourse of local identity, the presence of so many vacationing immigrants makes ferragosto a time when this issue is brought to the fore. As the piazza swells with local and visiting strollers, the residents make an effort to place their town in its best light. This is "Our Little Paris," their display suggests, "a modern and vibrant town." For their part, vacationing expatriots can content themselves with the knowledge that the cheques that they sent home over the years have not gone to waste and that their support has played at least a small part in the town's development.

Above all else the passeggiata is an event in which people come to be in close physical proximity with others, huddling in groups and walking arm in arm to reaffirm their interdependence. To stand alone during this collective display of public allegiance is to fundamentally forfeit the right to be a Sassano in the fullest sense of the term. The importance of sociability in the passeggiata is most clearly illustrated by the actions of Sasso's lone walker. This gentleman marches up and down the street with a rapid and mechanical gait; hurried and almost aggressive, he looks more like an exercise walker than a passeggiata stroller. He walks self-consciously and without style; his demeanor suggests heightened purposefulness – a compulsion. He seldom greets people, and other Sassani uniformly avert their gaze from him. In his frenetic, antisocial passeggio, the lone walker is the antithesis of the spirit of the Sassano passeggiata.

But the passeggiata is more than an image of communal sociability or uniform local identity; to the Sassani themselves, the passeggiata is a performance of village life, and each stroller's body is a medium for constituting representations of the local society as a whole. How can the individually pursued bodily activity of the strollers be understood as an intentional representation of the wider collectivity? While the individual participants use only their own body as a medium of expression, each individual understands that his or her actions will be interpreted in the context of all the other participants in the event, a context that includes representatives of almost every segment of Sassano society. Being in close physical proximity to people from all classes, ages, genders, marital statuses, and political affiliations in the town, the stroller's body is interpreted as neither an individual body nor part of a uniform group: it is seen as a part of an organization of bodies. In short, the common awareness of a totalizing context transforms the individual body into a member of society and individually pursued passeggiata performances become representations of the society as a whole.

The clearest way to illustrate this notion is through the idea of staking one's place. Individuals on the passeggiata symbolically stake their place in society by laying claim to the physical locations in the piazza. Elected officials, for example, frequently displayed their political power through passeggiata performance. Walking shoulder to shoulder from capo (head) to *quart da peda* (side by the feet), this chain of ten to twelve men would occupy the whole width of the street, dominating the entire piazza in a show of power and solidarity (figure 32). The men who mill about near the sidewalk bars usually turn and raise their heads to watch their politicians strolling in an unbroken line. Such a display would always change the dynamics of the event. The politicos' almost complete control of the street made

Figure 32   Politicos dominate the street (video still from the author's field tapes)

it difficult for other participants to pace at the rhythm at which they were accustomed, and many strollers chose the path of least resistance by walking around the politicians. During my first year of fieldwork, the local municipal corruption scandal was at its peak and Mayor Lantenari and his cronies were conspicuously absent from the promenade. Six months latter, the town had ousted Lantenari and elected a leader with socialist ties. On a return trip the following year, I observed Sassani glance with distrust as the new mayor strolled with members of the previous administration. In this context, the actors' use of space reflects their political power. By virtue of their position in the social hierarchy, Sassano politicians occupy a central place in the life of the town and the spatial dynamics they bring to the promenade reflect this reality. The sanguine self-confidence with which the politicians dominate the piazza acts as a forceful reminder to the townsfolk of the influence they exercise in village life.

If during the promenade political leaders conveyed their centrality in the community by commanding greater social space, Sassano widows communicated their marginality in society by operating on the sidelines. Typically, they enjoyed the proceedings from the edge of the street, the balconies, the terraces, or their front steps (figures 6 and 27). As chapter 4 explains, Italian widows are traditionally expected to abide by the ideals of female modesty; their lives have historically been restricted by religious doctrine, and their activities in the public sphere have been limited. Because of these longstanding social strictures, widows are seldom seen in the center of the piazza during the peak hours of the promenade. While the widow Maria, for example, thought it was unsuitable for a woman in her position to stroll on *il corso* (main thoroughfare), she hardly ever missed an occasion to sit on her balcony and watch the proceedings. On a nice day, she would typically lean against the railing to greet and converse with passersby. As a rule, she only would venture off into the piazza to do her morning's shopping or practice needlework in the villa (park).

While the widows reaffirm and embrace their marginalized role in Sasso by watching the passeggiata from the sideline, they also use their presence to assert the power of the marginal gaze. As the arbiters of propriety, they sit in judgment of the strollers on the street, their watchful eyes reminding those below literally and figuratively to *fare la strada diritta* (follow the straight and narrow path); the more boisterous shenanigans of the teenage boys and the more provocative performances of the adolescent women elicit their scolding remarks. By monitoring the conduct in the passeggiata, they stake a place for themselves in society and make sure that the traditional values of modesty and propriety still have some role in this new, modern Sasso. Though their age and special status in the community is in some ways limiting, it also affords them the luxury of bluntly expressing judgmental remarks or unpopular beliefs. Sassano teenagers, in fact, fear the reprisals of the older widows and the gossip that they wield so effectively. The coercive male gaze that women's studies scholars describe in their work has its counterpart in the equally powerful female gaze of the Sassano widows. This is not to say that Sasso is a feminist paradise; in fact, the rules of decorum that the widow's gaze upholds are often restrictive to women. To deny, however, the power that the widows do posses is equally to distort the situation. In the passeggiata performance, as in society, the margins are a location in the social continuum.

The physical centrality of the politicos and the marginality of the widows is an obvious metaphor for their positions in Sassano society, but not all staking of place in the promenade operates through proxemics. In fact, Sasso's actors use a wide array of expressive resources to carve a niche for themselves in village society. Most frequently, they do this by identifying with, co-opting, or reinterpreting the local values of civiltà, cosmopolitanism, and modernity.

In Sassano culture, the displays of urban sophistication are perhaps nowhere more evident then in the actions of the stylishly dressed female adolescents. Provocatively sashaying up and down the street with their coterie of friends, teenage girls on the passeggiata seek to

Figure 33   Anna (second from left) and her friends (video still from the author's field tapes)

affect airs of insouciance, coquettery, or mondaine worldliness. Anna, for example, evoked retro images with a 1960s crocheted hat and three-quarter-length stockings (figure 33). Her friend Dina could often be seen in a clinging knit top and skirt ensemble of lime green (figure 34). Wearing high-heeled shoes and a purse with a long narrow strap, her accessories came from a formal evening-wear collection. It is in the contrast between her ready-to-wear outfit and her formal accessories that the creativity of Dina's performance lay. With her long blond hair, sunglasses, and designer cigarette pants, Oriana evoked an urban, almost cinematic look (figure 35). Her thigh-length, unconstructed jacket was cinched at the waist and made of a dark blue crushed silk. While expensive clothing is a desiderata, bearing and demeanor are the crucial elements of passeggiata performance, and a skilled adolescent may conjure images of glamour and style with a simple flick of the wrist or a raising of the chin. Oriana supplemented the look of her elegant clothing by occasionally flipping her long blond mane back from her face in a gesture that was both studied and casual.

The teenagers are not the only ones who seek to emulate images from Italy's fashion magazines. Parading in conservative colors and tailored suits, a small but growing cadre of middle-aged professional women claim for themselves the values of social refinement and taste. Backgrounding the sexuality that the adolescents emphasize, these displays of sophistication link the broader cultural value of civility

Figure 34   Dina on the passeggiata (video still from the author's field tapes)

Figure 35   Oriana (video still from the author's field tapes)

to a distinctly female image of professional respectability. The jacket of Chiara's blue Chanel suit was made from a fine crushed wool; the conservative image that such designer fashions evoke was given individuality and daring by her dyed blond hair, beach-bronzed suntan, and heavy – but not gaudy – gold jewelry. Paola also wore a suit. Designed by Max Mara, the loose-fitting navy-blue gabardine draped her form nicely and allowed her to stroll with freedom and self-confidence. The suit mixes easily with a variety of tops and lets Paola look smart with a minimum of dressing time. Her low-healed walking shoes and short hair offer a similar opportunity for low-maintenance style. Shimmering slightly in the afternoon sunlight, Rina's white and blue striped sweater was crocheted from cotton and silk. Simple blue pants and matching pumps softened her look and made it more traditionally feminine. The kinesics of the professional women contain none of the signature affectations of the teenage girls. Their posture is upright but not stiff. With their relaxed shoulders and arms swinging loosely at their sides, their deportment is casual and suggests that they are at home, both in their bodies and in the community. Hoping to garner the respectability that the professionals have attainted, a number of women in their mid-twenties emulate this look.

In their piazza behavior, each of these three groups – widows, teenage girls, and middle-aged professionals – interpret social change in different ways. Whether they seek to be guardians of propriety, daring young moderns, or accomplished career women, all three reference the shifting gender roles of contemporary Italy and position themselves relative to the values of modernity and cosmopolitanism. In so doing they are not merely accomplishing *individual* social business, they are staking a place for their segment of the society in the wider culture. We are the widows, the watchful gaze of the older women announces, and we will make sure that our vision of modesty and respectability is adhered to in Sasso. We are the teenage women, the adolescents' display declares, and we have a place in this modern town. We are the career women, states the professionals' performance, and our social achievements must be recognized.

In the cinematic arc of the passeggiata, the displays of identity and the staking of place can reach great heights of nuance and detail. In sharp contrast, it is impossible to miss the disruptive antics of the motorini; in local usuage, the term "motorini" (literally, "mopeds") also refers to the teenage boys who favor these machines (figure 36). A source of constant annoyance to the other strollers, the motorini's rambunctious performance of masculine identity is an essential part of the dynamic street culture of Sasso. Without enough spending

Figure 36   The motorini (moped) boys (video still from the author's field tapes)

money to buy drinks at the cafés, they are relegated to the sidewalks; their favorite spot is a wide street corner across from one of the bigger bars along Corso Vittorio Emanuele. With their windbreakers, designer sunglasses, and gelled hair, the motorini lean against their bikes and watch the crowd go by. Smoking, scowling, ogling young women, and engaging in horseplay, these youths occasionally try to interfere with the rhythm of the strollers' passeggio by charging forward with their bikes or making noise. The revving of their motors and their boisterous, often incoherent yells frequently provoke shouts of anger from passersby. On busy days, the teens' view of the proceedings is often severely hampered by the sheer density of strollers in the street; outnumbered by pedestrians and incapable of looking across the park, the motorini boys would make a grand exit, roaring through the crowd in a noisy cavalcade.

Despite the motorini's disruptive antics, the walking hordes clearly controlled the piazza. Cowed by the dominant walkers, the adolescent males struggle to maintain their location in this public arena, withdrawing only when they are incapable of participating to their satisfaction. The motorini's behavior in the passeggiata reflects the larger social predicament that they face.

While women's roles have been partially expanded by the changes that have come to Sasso, males are still expected to fulfill the traditional roles of sexual instigator, breadwinner, and, eventually, father.

Well aware of Sasso's highly publicized corruption scandals and clientalistic hiring practices, the young men cannot feel that they have much chance to fulfill the economic expectations that the town has for them. On a more immediate level, Sasso's high youth unemployment and the limited entertainment venues for teenage boys leave them with a feeling of marginalization. Frustrated by their limited options, their conduct in the piazza reflects back to society the expectation that men will assert themselves in the public domain and behave in a sexually aggressive manner. Their tough fashions and disruptive antics allow the motorini to express a modern version of Italy's traditional male gender role and make their frustrations known. Relegated to the margins of the event and overwhelmed by the strolling mass of Sassani, the motorini are at least partially successful in staking a place for themselves in the local society.[8]

In each of these examples, we see participants on the passeggiata using their bodies as a medium of expression to make statements about their role in village life. While not every act in the piazza is meant as social commentary – sometimes going for a walk is just going for a walk – there is no doubt that people go into the piazza to see and be seen. Contextualized by representatives of every segment of Sassano society and oriented toward the perception of the town as a whole, bodily practices acquire the potential to be more than just a reflection of the individual's state of mind. Just as a figure cannot exist without a ground in visual perception, neither can an individual social role exist outside of a network of other social roles. Each one of the individual participants knows that their performing body will be a figure literally viewed against the ground of the piazza and metaphorically viewed against the ground of Sassano society writ large. As a result, individuals can use their bodily performances to comment upon their social identity and stake a place for themselves in the wider social structure. Taken together, these various "stakings of place" produce a representation of the entire, highly differentiated collectivity, a kind of kinetic sculpture of village life.

The purely structural features of the event allow such a systematic representation. The small area that the village occupies, the high population density (nearly three thousand inhabitants), and the general participation of the populace in the event guarantee that, on most nights, representatives of every strata and division of Sassano society are in attendance. The presence of such a representative sample allows the event to come to a kind of demographic critical mass. Physical features of the piazza also play a role here. The wide thoroughfare, deep sidewalks, omnipresent cafés, low balconies, bench-filled median strip, and gently sloping contour of *il corso* serve as the perfect arena for viewing others and marking social distinctions. Such structural features are a necessary but not a sufficient condition for creating the passeggiata's moving images of Sasso; it is the creative agency and sociological imagination of the townsfolk that achieves this kinetic sculpture. Each participant is a partial author, but that partial authoring is perceived and intended as constitutive of a systematic whole. Together with the demographics of the town and the architectural scale of the piazza, this ensemble of individual bodily practices become evocations – utopian, conservative, literal, radical, ironic, satiric – of Sassano society writ large.

6

Our Modernity

The goal of this study has been to explore how people use expressive culture to think about and negotiate the meanings of modernity. While the variety of traditional genres and mass-mediated forms that we have examined in chapters 3 and 4 all bear upon modernity, the passeggiata is the social sphere where these issues are made most palpable. Here, all of the concerns and misgivings about social progress are encapsulated and opened up for public debate. Changing gender roles, political corruption, industrialization, consumption – all of these themes are played out on the stage of the piazza. Where the court of public opinion or the local discourse surrounding the Twin Peaks scandal merely discuss the issues of modernity, the promenade does much more. Richly aesthetic, enacted through bodily practice, and collectively pursued, passeggiata performances allow Sassani to directly experience – however briefly – their differing visions of local identity and modernity. It is for this reason that Sassani treat the promenade as the centerpiece of the town's culture and that I have taken the promenade as my primary focus. Drawing together the various concerns of the previous chapters, this conclusion seeks to interpret Sassani's collective conversation about how modern lives may be led together.

We can begin by recalling that the Sassano passeggiata rose to prominence because of the social changes wrought by modernity in the postwar period. In the last forty years, the mass of Sassano residents have been transformed from contadini to impiegati – from farmers to factory workers enmeshed in the modern money economy.

With the rise of cheap consumer goods and ready-to-wear clothing, the impiegati for the first time had a wardrobe appropriate for public display, and the passeggiata was transformed from a weekly performance for the rich into a daily ritual of democratic equality and communal sociability.

As the passeggiata moved into the center of public life, it changed in other ways as well. Periods of social transformation often bring with them greater chances for social mobility, and the modernization of Sasso was no exception. With new possibilities for employment in the burgeoning industrial zone and a complex system of recommendations in the local politics, never had the opportunities for social advancement been so great or the pitfalls of social exclusion been so harrowing. While maintaining and establishing a public face is a universal feature of social life, the highly competitive atmosphere of the new Sasso brought great urgency to this project for all the townsfolk. The passeggiata rose to prominence as these social changes occurred, and, as a result, artistic display in the piazza became the main device for managing one's social identity. Understood in this way, the contemporary promenade is a culturally specific response to the social instabilities of modernity.

But the passeggiata is not just a by-product of larger historical forces. Sassani actively use the event to explore the meaning of modernity, and the event is about modernity in at least three distinct ways. First, as we have seen in the staking of place section, each segment of Sassano society invokes the concept of modernity in their performance to carve a niche for themselves in the town. Their performances do not merely reference the notion of modernity; they co-opt and reinterpret this idea, redefining their identities and creating new images of what their roles in modern life might be like. Perhaps what is most important is that in the passeggiata modernity is evoked through aesthetics; it is primarily images of sophistication and style (rather than wealth or technology) that Sassani identify with the modern and use in their performances.

For example, the female professionals' displays do not merely advocate for greater choices for women in a highly restrictive and patriarchal society, neither do their performances simply say that a town with modern pretensions must allow its women social equality; the career women lay claim to their hard-won opportunities and freedoms by creating highly aestheticized displays – displays of style, urban sophistication, civility, refinement, sartorial mastery, and effortless ease. In the passeggiata, such performances both legitimate their right to a career outside the home and serve as a unique statement of what being a modern, upper-middle-class woman might be like – professional and stylish, successful and disinvolto. Similarly, the adolescent females use experiments in fashion and the teenage males use raucous displays both to claim a position in the town ("Recognize us! We have urban style.") and to explore what their roles in modernity may be (daring and coquettish or aggressive and masculine).

Turning from the individual segments of Sassano society to the town's collective identity, one sees a second way in which the passeggiata is about modernity. Whether they are proud of their self-proclaimed cosmopolitanism or ashamed of their complicity, most of the townsfolk are committed to their identity, not just as career women or "moped" boys, but as residents of Sasso. As a result, much of the conduct in the passeggiata is a comment on the meaning of Sasso as a modern town, and the Sassani's ambivalent feelings toward their home echo the ambivalence that many of the great nineteenth-century social thinkers had toward modernity. In interviews, Sassani often depicted the passeggiata as a narcissistic display of capitalist consumption and vanity. Likewise, many Sassani feel the almost panoptic scrutiny of the passeggiata to be restrictive and constraining, an unpleasant reminder of the town's Byzantine politics. At the same time, Sassani also see the passeggiata as a sign of their town's civiltà and even the most cynical Sassani feel a measure of local pride when they enter the passeggiata zone. Here, representations of the promenade, representations of Sassano identity, and representations of modernity are inextricable mixed. Similar themes of pride and ambivalence were reflected in the postcards, *Giochi Senza Frontiere*, the local responses to *L'Istruttoria*, the folklore of village insults, and the rumors surrounding the Twin Peaks scandal.

The passeggiata is about modernity in one final sense. Not merely a public forum on village identity in the postwar period, the passeggiata is a collective meditation about the meaning of modernity itself. Here, Sassani reflect on their historical experiences and take stock of the radical social changes that have transformed both Sasso and the world. Such broad, even utopian, interpretations exceed even the bounds of the passeggiata and implicate all spheres of village cultural life. Like the modern Texans that Beverly Stoeltje and Richard Bauman describe, Sassani situate themselves "at the center of a macro-system, not in the periphery and ultimately reaffirm their capacity to comprehend the order of existence in the modern world in their own terms" (1989, 170). Returning to the themes of chapter 1, we can use Sassano ideas about modernity to gain new insights into North American culture and modernity in general.

The Sassani's visions of modernity must be understood in light of the massive outmigrations of Abruzzesi to North America during *la miseria* (literally, "the misery"; i.e., the period of economic and social devastation after the Second World War).[1] During these difficult days, fully one half of the population of Sasso left the town for the New World. As a result, North America plays a key role in Sasso's self-image. Through the eyes of Hollywood, America is the land of opportunity, boundless wealth, and progressive modernity. While the scholarship and literature of Americans of color have provided a critical corrective to this vision, the ethnography of those who chose not to join the "melting pot" can yield different perspectives.

To the Sassani who stayed, the Italy of the 1940s and 1950s was a devastated land, but also a land that could recover from the ravages of war. Today, their children see Sasso as a modernized small town, and, while Sassani do not deny that their home has its problems, their goal is to inhabit a modernity different from the modernity of America. If 1950s Hollywood saw America as the land of opportunity and of immigrants hungry for progress, Sassani often see America as the land of opportunism, of a rootless, historyless modernity, of European immigrants whose economic affluence came at the expense of *disinvoltura*, *civiltà*, and the arts of living. While Sassano discourse is marked by an ambivalence toward social change, we can see in the postcards and the best moments of the *passeggiata* a vision of an ideal Sasso and an understanding that there may be many different kinds of modernity. Neither premodern idyll nor alienated American metropolis, the townsfolk's ideal Sasso synthesizes the best of traditional Italian culture (stunning natural vistas, refined sociability, a cultivated aesthetic sense) with the best of the modern world (a developed economy, high-technology medicine, urbane cosmopolitanism). The Sassano ideal, in short, is a European modernity, a modernity that stands against what they see as the graceless and artless pragmatism of American culture. Exploring the ideal Sasso, we see a vision of America that is distinct from both the facile celebrations found in the films of Frank Capra and the critical views found in American and Canadian multicultural discourse. While it is commonly accepted that Emma Lazarus's inscription on the Statue of Liberty denies the suffering of people of color in the United States, it is less frequently acknowledged that the poem depicts all other countries as places of oppression and injustice. In the Sasso of the good *passeggiata*, I see a vision of Sassano identity – and by extension, a vision of America – that responds to this representation directly. "We are not huddled masses yearning to breathe free," the *passeggiata* seems to say, "and yours is not the only modernity. We have rebuilt our lives, and, while we have not made a paradise, our history is still being created. America is not our destiny: we are still building 'Our Little Paris.'"

Notes

CHAPTER ONE

1 The text of this poem was composed by Lino Venturi, a resident of Naples who frequently vacationed in Sasso. It was first performed during the talent show portion of Sasso's community games in the summer of 1994. For a discussion of the games, see chapter 3.

2 Many of the images I use to illustrate the passeggiata in this book were extracted from these field videotapes, and this accounts for their slightly grainy texture and poor resolution.

3 The negative images of il Mezzogiorno have provided ideological fodder for the Lega Nord (Northern League), a right-wing party that advocates Northern separatism. In response to attacks from the right, a number of Southern artists have begun to celebrate defiantly their Southern identity. Using regional dialectics in their work, musicians such as Pino Daniele or the members of the band Nuovi Briganti (see Plastino 1996) and film-makers like Gabriele Salvatores challenge the simplistic stereotypes of Southern laziness and corruption. In Italy today there are also Southern intellectuals who try to highlight their North African heritage by emphasizing the relationships between their culture and that of the thousands of immigrants who have come to Italy from Morocco, Senegal, and Tunisia.

4 It is interesting to note that even in the early period of modern Abruzzese outmigration, people from the province traveled to the most far flung parts of the world. For example, Mario Arpea's study of 1880s Roccodimezzo (1997), a hilltop village in Aquila (a region within the Abruzzo),

reveals that the destinations for outmigration included Siberia, Alaska, Patagonia, and Indochina.

5 For a discussion of the devastation of the small town of Lama dei Peligni, see Del Negro (1997).

6 Literally, clerk; in everyday talk the term is used to mean wage earner, a worker in the money economy.

7 It is important to note that during the early period there were different types of remigration. As ethnic studies scholar Joe Feagin points out, some of the late nineteenth and early twentieth century Italian immigrants "were temporary sojourners, sometimes termed 'birds of paradise,' whose aim was to make money in the United States and then return to Italy to invest in enterprises at home" (Feagin 1984, 110). Others, however, expected their stays to be longer but planned to return in the more distant future. Likewise in the second wave of migration, there was also a mix of "birds of paradise," long-term reimmigrants, and immigrants.

8 For regional statistics on post–Second World War Italian emigration and return, see Russell King's *Il ritorno in patria: Return Migration to Italy in Historical Perspective* (1988).

9 This is a term Italian immigrants and the families they left behind use to refer to the United States and Canada. Older Sassani residents would also occasionally use this expression to refer to both Latin America and South America.

10 Although Sasso fares well in terms of overall quality of life, a third of its residents are over sixty-five (Passarelli 1998, 65), and there are many teenagers in the community who feel that the quiet rhythm of village life is lacking in excitement.

11 For a rich discussion of the role of civiltà in Italian culture, see Silverman (1975).

12 Another metagenre into which the passeggiata could be fitted is what Dorothy Noyes calls "facade performances" (1996), a broad category that includes such expressive forms as the serenade, the luck-visit, and mumming. The term "facade" here is used in two senses, to indicate the fact that these performances occur before architectural fronts and that they deal with the issue of respectability – an individual's or group's social facade. Here, members of different classes gaze upon one another and evaluate each other's position in the local hierarchy. In as much as the passeggiata takes place in a specifically demarcated public space and often deals with the issue of reputation, this event could be considered a facade performance. The fit is imperfect, however. In terms of expressive practices, the passeggiata takes place before a series of architectural fronts, but it also occurs within the open space of the piazza and in the pastoral setting of the villa park. And while reputations are frequently negotiated in the passeggiata, this event is about much more than respectability. Among many things, the passeggiata is a venue for honing and

displaying aesthetic skills, a place of artful conversation and pleasant interaction. Perhaps most importantly, the passeggiata is, for Sassani, the arena par excellence in which individuals and groups contemplate and debate the meaning of modernity and their place within it.

13 Discussing similar patterns of development in a Latin American context, Setha Low observes that public spaces like piazzas and plazas developed historically as sites for public sociability and continue today to serve as arenas of aesthetic and political expression. While the architectural and cultural history of the piazza is a fascinating topic, my focus here is on the contemporary usage of the piazza in a central Italian town, rather than the chain of past events that lead up to it. For a more detailed analysis of the politics and the history of the public square, see Setha Lowe (2000), Michael Webb (1990), and Paul Zucker (1959).

14 The Irish Bowery girls of New York at the turn of the century had much in common with Sasso's female passeggiata strollers (Del Negro 1999). For a discussion of nineteenth-century bourgeois promenading in New York, see Scobey (1992).

15 See Nardini (1997) for a rich analysis of the notion of *bella figura* in an Italian-American context.

16 In a related vein, see Featherstone's discussion of impression management and the act of consumption (1991).

CHAPTER TWO

1 A similar pattern can be found in the work of Karl Marx. While Marx was, of course, critical of capitalism, he reserved a special admiration for industry's ability to mobilize the forces of nature. Like the other great nineteenth-century social thinkers, Marx did not reject technological innovation; he merely condemned the exploitative uses to which it is put in capitalist society.

2 The notion of authenticity in folklore studies has been richly explored by Regina Bendix (1997). Though her focus is on authenticity rather than modernity, she argues that romantic nineteenth-century folklorists took the search for the "authentically" premodern peasantry as their primary methodological imperative, and Bendix's work is critical for anyone interested in the history of the discipline.

3 For a rich critique of the simplistic celebration of social struggle, see Lila Abu-Lughod (1990).

4 A number of other scholarly traditions have influenced my interest in the informal spheres of social interaction. In *The Practice of Everyday Life*, Michel de Certeau (1984) provides an important analysis of the subtle logic of ordinary conduct. Examining activities such as walking or stealing company property, de Certeau treats mundane practices as "tactical" (8) responses to larger social forces. Focusing on everyday bodily practices

such as grooming, strolling, and spectating, I hope to provide ethnographic detail to inform and enrich de Certeau's largely theoretical study. Another source of inspiration for my research is the work of Jonas Frykman and Orvar Löfgren (1987). In their historical ethnology, they shed light on the development of middle-class culture in Sweden by examining the complex ideologies that surround quotidian practices of hygiene, leisure, and domestic life. While broader in scope, Fernand Braudel's (1972) classic study of Mediterranean social history also reveals a concern for understanding how everyday cultural practices from the past fundamentally structure contemporary social life.

5 By "style" I mean an ensemble of expressive means that includes posture, gait, clothing, kinesics, and proxemics. In Goffman's work the term demeanor is used to denote a similar group of phenomena and refers to deportment, dress, and bearing. In a related vein, Hebdige describes subcultural style as a synthesis of argot, costume, and attitude (Hebdige 1988).

6 See Synott and Howes (1992) for an excellent intellectual history of scholarship on the body.

7 Aggressive performances of male prowess and control, however, are not always indicators of social power. As Muriel Dimen and Ernestine Friedl's work suggests (1976), Greek men's highly visible and prestigious displays such as dancing, singing, and drinking might actually serve to obscure feelings of powerlessness.

8 A predecessor of both of these traditions can be found in the well-established genre of expatriate writing that exists in Western literature in general and American literature in particular. The French sociologist Alexis De Tocqueville is famous for his massive treatise on American society, *Democracy in America* (1966 [1835]), while more recently the Italian journalist Beppe Severgnini brought a European gaze to bear on American culture (2002). The traditional role of writers such as these has been to provide a unique and even whimsical perspective on North American life. While there is a substantial body of work by literary expatriates from Canada and the United States, there are few studies that explore the visions of North America held by natives of foreign countries. My research seeks to reverse this traditional paradigm in Canadian and American studies by examining what the ethnographic encounter abroad can tell us about life here at home. In the field, my interactions with others provided me with an opportunity for understanding how Italians constructed my North American identity. Fluid and shifting, these representations illustrate the highly contextual quality of cultural labels. This phenomenon has been widely noted in folklore scholarship. For example, Richard Bauman's classic article "Differential Identity and the Social Base of Folklore" (1972) argues that a people's sense of who they are is frequently developed in opposition to other groups within society. In

recent years, contemporary folklorists and historians of ethnicity have focused special scrutiny on these issues (Klymasz 1973; Gans 1979; Sollers 1989; Goral et al. 1990; Del Giudice 1993; Handler 1994). As Stephen Stern and John Cicala argue (1991), identity is always selectively manipulated and reinterpreted in response to the needs of the situated social context. Before all of this, the pioneering work of Américo Paredes (1958) captures these dynamics at play in the border culture between Texas and Mexico.

In Sasso my insider/outsider status provided me with a perspective uniquely suited to exploring the various facets of Italian and North American culture. This study is an examination of the experience of "double consciousness" (Du Bois 1994) that, to some extent, all ethnographers encounter in the field. I hope to show how my intellectual life grew out of my own ethnic experience and the chronic sense of otherness so important to that experience. Drawing on these various reflexive and expatriate literary traditions, I hope to turn the musings of an immigrant daughter into a humanistic investigation of culture, social change, and gender.

9 A somewhat different strain of reflexive research can be found among folklorists and linguistic anthropologists engaged in the ethnography of speaking (Hymes 1975; Bauman 1988; Briggs 1993). A central program of this work is to illuminate the indexical and metapragmatic means by which folklore texts are tied to the ongoing performance event. Because performers often reference their folklorist interlocutors in the performance and may tailor their text to their perception of their audience's expectations, contemporary work in this field often contains a substantial reflexive component.

CHAPTER THREE

1 Often, the tourist literature represents this isolation as the source of the Abruzzo's unsullied environment and its anachronistic, almost pagan culture. For example, a writer for *The American Way*, the American Airlines inflight magazine, begins his romantic portrayal of the Abruzzo by suggesting that, "Because it was cut off from the rest of Italy for centuries by formidable mountain ranges, Abruzzo remains a mysterious place, which adds to its allure. The people are still superstitious, mounting extravagant religious festivals built around cabalistic numbers, and the spoken dialect remains strong, even as others slip away into modern Italian" (Mariani 1998, 44).

2 For an analysis of postcards and tourist literature, see Löfgren (1991).

3 The animosity that some Sassani have expressed toward these "summer people" may be grounded in class tensions, some argue; others, however, have suggested that these Sassani are shamed by the fact that it took outsiders to restore Sasso's historic buildings.

4 For the text of the poem, see the epigraph to chapter 1.

5 This response is what Herzfeld describes as a kind of productive eghois-mos (self-regard), "a social stance to be adopted in [a] hostile and imperfect world" (Herzfeld 1987, 127).

CHAPTER FOUR

1 For essays on television serials produced in Latin America, Asia, and Africa, see Robert C. Allen's *To Be Continued: Soap Operas Around the World* (1995).

CHAPTER FIVE

1 For an explanation of my use of the word "aesthetic" see chapter 1, n. 4.

2 Related phenomena are described by Dorothy Noyes in her work on costume in the public spaces of late-eighteenth-century Madrid. Sites such as the Prado gardens, the theater, and the bullfights, Noyes reports, brought members of different classes together and provided them with occasions for studying each other's conduct and appearance (Noyes 1998). Noyes argues that "this exchange of gazes led to the exchange of custom and to what Ortega y Gasset (1958) calls a 'deliberate stylization' of culture" (Noyes 1998, 198). Just as the residents of Madrid imitated the gestures and poses of celebrated theater actors, so too do today's young Sassano women who borrow their looks from the pages of fashion magazines and images of the movies.

3 These ideas connect with themes we have explored in chapter 4. As we saw, in traditional Italian culture, women were seen as possessing an overwhelming sexual power that they alone are responsible for containing. In the context of these beliefs, it is not surprising that all female performances in the passeggiata, except those of the oldest women, are to some degree sexualized.

4 While gender segregation certainly exists in the piazza during the passeggiata (with the balconies and terraces largely populated by women and the bars and cafés almost exclusively reserved for men) it would be a mistake to think that these groups exist in isolated social worlds. It is true that in Sasso the passeggiata is often viewed as a female-centered pastime; however, men are allowed to perform in this arena and frequently do so. More importantly, the passeggiata is about seeing and being seen, and both men and women come to this event in order to gaze at one another, making the gendered spaces of the piazza permeable and interactive.

5 For a rich discussion of the notion of *bella figura* in an Italian-American context, see Nardini (1999).

6 The "distracted walker" is a perfect illustration of what Dell Hymes has described as a "performance in the perfunctory key, in which the

responsibility for a display of communicative competence is undertaken out of a sense of cultural duty, traditional obligation, but offering . . . little pleasure or enhancement of experience" (Bauman 1977, 26).

7 As I shall suggest below, Sassani represent the act of interpreting the character of the other as both the rational process of piecing together bits of information and an almost supernatural phenomenon that arises in a flash of second sight. In this way, Sassani's interpretive practices bear a striking resemblance to the deciphering of tea leaves or tarot cards. In all three situations, the interpreter treats the world as meaningful ensemble of signs that careful inspection and serendipity may convert into knowledge and wisdom. Such a process is primarily visual and sensual rather than linguistic. It is for this reason that I have chosen the term bodily "divination," rather than "reading" or "interpreting" the body, to describe Sassani's interpretive acts.

8 On the position of adolescent males in industrial society, see Willis (1977), Tricarico (1991), Weinstein (1991).

CHAPTER SIX

1 Loaded with derogatory implications, the word "miseria" has often been used to invoke the stereotype of Italians as a rural, backward people who live in a world where only the devious and cunning survive. Despite the negative connotation, I have retained the term because it was the word Sassani most commonly used to describe the economic hardship of post–Second World War Italy.

Bibliography

Abrahams, Roger D. 1968. "Introductory Remarks to a Rhetorical Theory of Folklore." In *Journal of American Folklore*, vol. 81, no. 320: 143–57.

– 1970. *Deep Down in the Jungle ...: Negro Narrative Folklore from the Streets of Philadelphia*. Chicago: Aldine Publishing Company.

– 1975. "Negotiating Respect: Patterns of Presentation among Black Women." In *Women and Folklore: Images and Genres*, edited by Claire R. Farrer, 58–61. Prospects Heights, IL: Waveland Press.

– 1981. "Shouting Match at the Border: The Folklore of Display Events." In *"And other neighborly names ...": Social Process and Cultural Image in Texas Folklore*, edited by Richard Bauman and Roger D. Abrahams, 303–21. Austin: University of Texas Press.

Abu-Lughod, Janet. 1997. "Going beyond Global Babble." In *Culture, Globalization, and the World-System: Contemporary Conditions for the Representations of Identity*, edited by Anthony King, 131–8. Minneapolis: University of Minnesota Press.

Abu-Lughod, Lila. 1990. "The Romance of Resistance." In *American Ethnologist*, vol. 17, no. 1: 41–55.

– 1991. "Writing against Culture." In *Recapturing Anthropology*, edited by Richard Fox, 137–62. Santa Fe: School of American Research Press.

Ammons, Elizabeth. 1986. "The Engineer as Cultural Hero and Willa Cather's First Novel, *Alexander's Bridge*." In *American Quarterly*, vol. 38, no. 5: 746–60.

Ann, L. 1994. "Due testimoni: Ylenia è viva." In *Corriere della sera*, 2 February 1994: 13.

Appadurai, Arjun. 1996. *Modernity at Large: Cultural Dimensions of Globalization*. Minneapolis: University of Minnesota Press.

Ardener, Shirley, ed. 1975. *Perceiving Women*. New York: Wiley.

– 1993. *Women and Space: Ground Rules and Social Maps.* Providence: Berg.

Argyle, Michael. 1975. *Bodily Communication.* New York: International University Press.

– 1976. *Gaze and Mutual Gaze.* Cambridge: Cambridge University Press.

Arpea, Mario. 1987. *Alle origini dell'emigrazione Abruzzese: La vicenda dell'Altipiano delle Rocche.* Milano: Franco Angeli.

Babcock, Barbara, ed. 1978. *The Reversible World: Symbolic Inversion in Art and Society.* New York: Cornell University Press.

Banfield, Edward. 1958. *The Moral Basis of a Backward Society.* Glencoe: Free Press.

Barber, Karin. 1987. "Popular Arts in Africa." In *African Studies Review,* vol. 30, no. 3: 1–18.

Barzini, Luigi Giorgio. 1964. *The Italians.* New York: Athenaeum.

Baudrilliard, Jean. 1988. *America.* Translated by Chris Turner. New York: Verso.

Bauman, Richard. 1972. "Differential Identity and the Social Base of Folklore." In *Toward New Perspectives in Folklore,* edited by Américo Paredes and Richard Bauman, 31–41. Austin: University of Texas Press.

– 1977. *Verbal Art as Performance.* Prospect Heights, IL: Waveland Press.

– 1983. "Folklore and the Forces of Modernity." In *Folklore Forum,* vol. 16, no. 2: 153–8.

Behar, Ruth and Deborah A. Gordon. 1995. *Women Writing Culture.* Berkeley: University of California Press.

Ben-Amos, Dan. 1972. "Toward a Definition of Folklore in Context." In *Toward New Perspectives in Folklore,* edited by Américo Paredes and Richard Bauman, 3–15. Austin: University of Texas Press.

Bendix, Regina. 1997. *In Search of Authenticity: The Formation of Folklore Studies.* Madison: University of Wisconsin Press.

Benjamin, Walter. 1989. *The Dialectics of Seeing: Walter Benjamin and the Arcades Project,* edited by Susan Buck Morss. Cambridge: MIT Press.

Benthall, Jonathan and Ted Polhemus. 1975. *The Body as a Medium of Expression.* London: Allen Lane.

Berger, Harris M. and Giovanna P. Del Negro. 2002. "Bauman's *Verbal Art* and the Social Organization of Attention: The Role of Reflexivity in the Aesthetics of Performance." In *Journal of American Folklore,* vol. 115, no. 455: 62–91.

– 2004. *Identity and Everyday Life: Essays in the Study of Folklore, Music, and Popular Culture.* Middletown, CT: Wesleyan University Press.

Birdwhistle, Ray L. 1972. *Kinesics and Context: Essays on Body Motion Communication.* New York: Ballantine.

Bohlen, Celestine. 1996. "Italy's North-South Gap Widens, Posing Problem for Europe, Too." In *The New York Times,* 15 November 1996: A1-A8.

Bolino, Giuseppe. 1973. *La spopolazione dell'Abruzzo: Aspetti sociologici dell'emigrazione regionale.* Lanciano: Itinerari.

Borland, Katherine. 1991. "'That's not what I said': Interpretative Conflict in Oral Narrative Research." In *Women's Words: The Feminist Practice of Oral*

History, edited by Sherna Berger Gluck and Daphne Patai, 63–76. New York: Routledge.

Botkin, B.A. 1944. *A Treasury of American Folklore: Stories, Ballads, and Traditions of the People.* New York: Crown Publishers.

Braudel, Fernand. 1972. *The Mediterranean and the Mediterranean World in the Age of Philip II.* Translated by Siân Reynolds. New York: Harper & Row.

Briggs, Charles L. 1988. *Competence in Performance: The Creativity of Tradition in Mexicano Verbal Art.* Philadelphia: University of Pennsylvania Press.

Brownmiller, Susan. 1984. *Femininity.* New York: Linden Press/Simon & Schuster.

Bull, Ann Cento. 2001. "Social and Political Cultures in Italy from 1860 to the Present Day." In *The Cambridge Companion to Modern Italian Culture,* edited by Zygmunt G. Baranski and Rebecca J. West, 35–62. Cambridge: Cambridge University Press.

Cashmore, E. Ellis. 1987. "Shades of Black, Shades of White." In *Popular Music and Communication,* edited by James Lull, 245–65. New York: Sage Publications.

Castiglione, Baldassare. 1976 [1528]. *The Book of the Courtier.* Translated by George Bull. Harmondsworth: Penguin Books.

Clifford, James and George E. Marcus. 1986. *Writing Culture: The Poetics and Politics of Ethnography.* Berkeley: University of California Press.

Coombe, Rosemary. 1990. "Barren Ground: Re-conceiving Honour and Shame in the Field of Mediterranean Ethnography." In *Anthropologia,* vol. 32, no. 2: 221–38.

Corsaro, William A. 1990. "Disputes in the Peer Culture of American and Italian Nursery School Children." In *Conflict and Talk,* edited by Alan Grimshaw, 21–66. Cambridge: Cambridge University Press.

– 1994. "Discussion, Debate, and Friendship Processes: Peer Discourse in U.S. and Italian Nursery Schools." In *Sociology of Education,* vol. 67, no. 1: 1–26.

Corsaro, William A. and Thomas Rizzo. 1988. "Discussione and Friendship: Socialization Processes in the Peer Culture of Italian Nursery School Children." In *American Sociological Review,* vol. 53, no. 6: 879–94.

Cowan, Jane. 1990. *Dance and the Body Politic in Northern Greece.* Princeton: Princeton University Press.

Crapanzano, Vincent. 1980. *Tuhami: Portrait of a Moroccan.* Chicago: The University of Chicago Press.

Csikszentmihalyi, Mihaly. 2000 [1975]. *Beyond Boredom and Anxiety.* San Francisco: Jossey-Bass Publishers.

Davis, Susan G. 1986. *Parades and Power: Street Theatre in Nineteenth-Century Philadelphia.* Philadelphia: Temple University Press.

De Bernardi, Alberto. 1994. "Clientelismo." In *Stato dell'Italia,* edited by Paul Ginsborg, 83–6. Milano: Bruno Mondadori.

de Certeau, Michel. 1984. *The Practice of Everyday Life.* Translated by Steven Rendall. Berkeley: University of California Press.

De Martino, Marco. 1994. "Ylenia dei misteri." In *Panorama*, 11 February 1994: 12–16.

De Tocqueville, Alexis. 1966. *Democracy in America*, edited by J.P. Mayer and Max Lerner. Translated by George Lawrence. New York: Harper & Row.

Del Giudice, Luisa. 1993. *Studies in Italian American Folklore*. Logan: Utah State University Press

Del Negro, Giovanna. 1997. *Looking through My Mother's Eyes: Life Stories of Nine Italian Immigrant Women in Canada*. Toronto: Guernica Editons.

– 2000. "*Passeggiata*." In *The Italian American Experience: An Encyclopedia*, edited by Salvatore LaGumina et al., 446–7. New York: Garland Publications, Inc.

Del Negro, Giovanna P. and Harris M. Berger. 2001. "Character Divination and Kinetic Sculpture in the Central Italian Passeggiata (Ritual Promenade): Interpretive Frameworks and Expressive Practices from a Body-Centered Perspective." In *Journal of American Folklore*, vol. 114, no. 451: 5–19.

Dégh, Linda. 1989 [1969]. *Folktales and Society: Storytelling in a Hungarian Peasant Community*. Translated by Emily M. Schossberger. Bloomington: Indiana University Press.

– 1975. "The Study of Ethnicity in Modern European Ethnology." In *Journal of the Folklore Institute*, vol. 12, no. 2/3: 113–29.

– 1994. *American Folklore and the Mass Media*. Bloomington: Indiana University Press.

Denby, Priscilla. 1971. "Folklore in the Mass Media." In *Folklore Forum*, vol. 4, no. 5: 113–25.

Dickie, John. 2001. "The Notion of Italy." In *The Cambridge Companion to Modern Italian Culture*, edited by Zygmunt G. Baranski and Rebecca J. West, 17–34. Cambridge: Cambridge University Press.

Dimen, Muriel and Ernestine Friedl, eds. 1976. *Regional Variation in Modern Greece and Cyprus*. New York: New York Academy of Sciences.

Dorson, Richard Mercer. 1971. "Is There a Folk in the City?" In *The Urban Experience and Folk Tradition*, edited by Américo Paredes and Ellen Steckert, 21–64. Austin: University of Texas Press.

Dorson, Richard Mercer, ed. 1972. *Folklore and Folklife: An Introduction*. Chicago: University of Chicago Press.

Dorson, Richard Mercer. 1981. *Land of the Mill Rats*. Cambridge: Harvard University Press.

Du Bois, W.E.B. 1994. *The Souls of Black Folk*. New York: Dover Publications, Inc.

Dubisch, Jill, ed. 1986. *Gender and Power in Rural Greece*. Princeton: Princeton University Press.

Dundes, Alan. 1977. "Who Are the Folk?" In *Frontiers of Folklore*, edited by William Bascom, 17–35. Boulder: Westview Press.

Dundes, Alan and Alessandro Falassi. 1975. *La Terra in Piazza: An Interpretation of the Palio of Siena.* Berkeley: University of California Press.

Dundes, Alan and Carl R. Pagter, eds. 1978. *Work Hard and You Shall Be Rewarded: Urban Folklore from the Paperwork Empire.* Bloomington: Indiana University Press.

Durkheim, Emile. 1964. *The Division of Labor in Society.* Translated by George Simpson. New York: The Free Press.

Eakins, Barbara Westbrook and R. Gene Eakins. 1978. *Sex Differences in Human Communication.* Boston: Houghton Mifflin.

Eisenstadt, S.N. 2000. "Multiple Modernities." In *Daedalus*, vol. 129, no. 1: 1–30.

Ellis, Carolyn and Arthur P. Bochner. 2000. "Autoethnography, Personal Narrative, Reflexivity: Researcher as Subject." In *Handbook of Qualitative Research*, edited by Norman K. Denzin and Yvonna S. Lincoln, 733–68. Thousand Oaks, CA: Sage Publications.

Fabian, Johannes. 1978. "Popular Culture in Africa: Findings and Conjectures." In *Africa*, vol. 48, no. 4: 315–34.

Farrer, Claire R., ed. 1975. *Women and Folklore: Images and Genres.* Prospect Heights, IL: Waveland Press.

Falassi, Alessandro. 1980. *Folklore by the Fireside.* Austin: University of Texas Press.

– 1987. "Festival: Definition and Morphology." In *Time out of Time*, edited by Alessandro Falassi, 1–10. Alburqueque: University of New Mexico Press.

Feagin, Joe R. 1984. *Racial and Ethnic Relations.* New Jersey: Prentice Hall, Inc.

Featherstone, Mike, ed. 1990. *Global Culture: Nationalism, Globalization, and Modernity.* London: Sage Publications.

Featherstone, Mike, Mike Hepworth, and Bryan S. Turner, eds. 1991. *The Body: Social Process and Cultural Theory.* London: Sage Publications.

Felice, Costantino. 1989. *Il disagio di vivere: Il cibo, la casa, le malattie in Abruzzo e Molise dall'unità al secondo dopoguerra.* Milano, Italy: Franco Angeli.

Figgen, Kathleen L. 1990. *Miracles and Promises: Popular Religious Cults and Saints in Argentina.* Ph.D. dissertation, Indiana University.

Fine, Elizabeth C. 1984. *The Folklore Text: From Performance to Print.* Bloomington: Indiana University Press.

Forgacs, David and Robert Lumley, eds. 1996. *Italian Cultural Studies: An Introduction.* Oxford: Oxford University Press.

Friedman, Jonathan. 1990. "Being in the World: Globalization and Localization." In *Global Culture: Nationalism, Globalization, and Modernity,* edited by Mike Featherstone, 311–28. London: Sage Publications.

– 1995. "Global System, Globalization, and the Parameters of Modernity." In *Global Modernities*, edited by Mike Featherstone et al., 69–90. London: Sage Publications.

Frykman, Jonas and Orvar Löfgren. 1987. *The Culture Builders: A Historical Anthropology of Middle-Class Life.* Translated by Alan Crozier. New Brunswick: Rutgers University Press.

Gans, Herbert J. 1979. "Symbolic Ethnicity: The Future of Ethnic Groups and Cultures in America." In *On the Making of Americans*, edited by Herbert J. Gans, 193–221. Philadelphia: University of Pennsylvania Press.

Gaonkar, Dilip Parameshwar. 1999. "On Alternative Modernities." In *Public Culture*, vol. 11, no. 1: 1–19.

Georges, Robert and Michael Owen Jones. 1980. *People Studying People: The Human Element in Fieldwork*. Berkeley: University of California Press.

Giddens, Anthony. 1990. *The Consequences of Modernity.* Cambridge: Polity Press.

Ginsborg, Paul. 1990. *A History of Contemporary Italy: Society and Politics, 1943– 1988*. London: Penguin Books.

– 1994. "Familismo." In *Stato dell'Italia*, edited by Paul Ginsborg, 78–82. Milano: Mondadori.

Gitlin, Todd. 1983. *Inside Prime Time*. New York: Pantheon Books.

Glassie, Henry H., Edward D. Ives, and John F. Szwed. 1970. *Folksongs and Their Makers*. Bowling Green: Popular Press.

Glassie, Henry H. 1982. *Passing the Time in Ballymenone: Culture and History of an Ulster Community.* Philadelphia: University of Pennsylvania Press.

Goffman, Erving. 1959. *The Presentation of Self in Everyday Life*. New York: Doubleday Press.

– 1961. *Encounters: Two Studies in the Sociology of Interaction*. Indianapolis: Bobbs Merrill.

– 1967. *Interaction Ritual: Essays on Face-to-Face Behavior.* New York: Anchor.

– 1972. *Strategic Interaction*. New York: Ballantine.

– 1983. "The Interaction Order: American Sociological Association 1982 Presidential Address." In *American Sociological Review*, vol. 48, no. 1: 1–7.

Goodwin, Joseph P. 1989. *More Man than You'll Ever Be: Gay Folklore and Acculturation in Middle America*. Bloomington: Indiana University Press.

Gribaudi, Gabriella. 1993. "Familismo e famiglie a Napoli e nel Mezzogiorno." In *Meridiana*, vol. 17, no. 17: 13–41.

Hall, Edward T. 1966. *The Hidden Dimension*. New York: Doubleday.

Hall, Judith. 1984. *Nonverbal Sex Differences: Communication Accuracy and Expressive Style*. Baltimore: Johns Hopkins University Press.

Hall, Stuart, David Held, Don Hubert, and Kenneth Thompson, eds. 1996. *Modernity: An Introduction to Modern Societies*. London: Blackwell.

Handler, Richard. 1988. *Nationalism and the Politics of Culture in Quebec*. Madison: University of Wisconsin Press.

– 1994. "Is 'Identity' a Useful Cross-cultural Concept?" In *Commemorations: The Politics of National Identity*, edited by John R. Gillis, 27–40. Princeton: Princeton University Press.

Hannerz, Ulf. 1987. "The World in Creolization." In *Africa*, vol. 57, no. 4: 546–59.

– 1990. "Cosmopolitans and Locals in World Culture." In *Global Culture: Nationalism, Globalization, and Modernity,* edited by Mike Featherstone, 237– 51. London: Sage Publications.

– 1997. "Scenarios for Peripheral Cultures." In *Culture, Globalization, and the World-System: Contemporary Conditions for the Representation of Identity*, edited by Anthony King, 107–28. Minneapolis: University of Minnesota Press.

Harvey, David. 2000. "Time-Space Compression and the Postmodern Condition." In *The Global Transformations Reader*, edited by David Held and Anthony McGrew, 82–91. Cambridge: Polity Press.

Hebdige, Dick. 1988. *Subculture: The Meaning of Style*. London: Routledge.

Henley, Nancy and Jo Freeman. 1995. "The Sexual Politics of Interpersonal Behavior." In *Women: A Feminist Perspective*, edited by Jo Freeman, 457–69. Mountain View, CA: Mayfield Publishing Company.

Herder, Johann Gottfried von. 1992. *Selected Early Works, 1764–1767*. Translated by Ernest A. Menze with Michael Palma. University Park: Pennsylvania State University Press.

Herzfeld, Michael. 1980. "Honor and Shame: Some Problems in the Comparative Analyses of Moral Systems." In *Man*, vol. 15, no. 2: 339–51.

– 1985. *The Poetics of Manhood: Contest and Identity in a Cretan Mountain Village*. Princeton: Princeton University Press.

– 1987. *Anthropology through the Looking-Glass: Critical Ethnography in the Margins of Europe*. New York: Cambridge University Press.

– 1991. "Silence, Submission, and Subversion: Toward a Poetics of Womanhood." In *Contested Identities: Gender and Kinship in Modern Greece*, edited by Peter Loisos and Evthymios Papataziarchis, 79–97. Princeton: Princeton University Press.

Hymes, Dell. 1975. "Folklore's Nature and the Sun's Myth." In *Journal of American Folklore*, vol. 88, no. 350: 345–69.

Ives, Edward D. 1993 [1964]. *Larry Gorman: The Man Who Made the Songs*. Fredericton, NB: Goose Lane Editions.

Jones, Ernest. 1965. "Pyschonanalysis and Folklore." In *The Study of Folklore*, edited by Alan Dundes, 88–102. Englewood Cliffs, NJ: Prentice-Hall, Inc.

Jordon, Rosan A. and Susan J. Kalcik, eds. 1985. *Women's Folklore, Women's Culture*. Philadelphia: University of Pennsylvania Press.

Kapchan, Deborah. 1994. "Moroccan Female Performers Defining the Social Body." In *Journal of American Folklore*, vol. 107, no. 423: 82–105.

King, Russell. 1988. *Il ritorno in patria: Return Migration to Italy in Historical Perspective*. Durham: University of Durham Geography Department.

Kirshenblatt-Gimblett, Barbara. 1975. "A Parable in Context." In *Folklore: Performance and Communication*, edited by Dan Ben-Amos and Kenneth S. Goldstein, 350–77. The Hague: Mouton.

Klymasz, Robert B. 1973. "From Immigrant to Ethnic Folklore: A Canadian View of Process and Transition." In *Journal of the Folklore Institute*, vol. 10, no. 3: 131–9.

Korson, George Gershon. 1938. *Minstrels of the Mine Patch: Songs and Stories of the Anthracite Industry*. Hatboro, PA: Folklore Associates.

– 1943. *Coal Dust on the Fiddle: Songs and Stories of the Bituminous Industry.* Philadelphia: University of Pennsylvania Press.

Kratz, Corrine. 1990. "Persuasive Suggestions and Reassuring Promises: Emergent Parallelism and Dialogic Encouragement in Song." In *Journal of American Folklore*, vol. 103, no. 407: 42–67.

Lakoff, George. 1987. *Women, Fire, and Dangerous Things*. Chicago: University of Chicago Press.

Lawless, Elaine J. 1992. "'I was afraid someone like you ... an outsider ... would misunderstand': Negotiating Interpretative Differences between Ethnographers and Subjects." In *Journal of American Folklore*, vol. 105, no. 417: 302–14.

Leal, Ondina Fachel and George Ruben Oliven. 1988. "Class Interpretation of Soap Opera Narrative: The Case of the Brazilian Novela, 'Summer Sun.'" In *Theory, Culture, and Society*, vol. 5, no. 1: 81–99.

Lemann, Nicholas. 1996. "Kicking in Groups." In *Atlantic Monthly*, April 1996: 22–6.

Limón, José. 1994. *Dancing with the Devil: Society and Cultural Poetics in Mexican-American South Texas*. Madison: University of Wisconsin Press.

Low, Setha M. 2000. *On the Plaza: The Politics of Public Space and Culture.* Austin: University of Texas Press.

Magli, Patrizia. 1989. "Face and the Soul." In *Fragments of a History of the Human Body, Part II*, edited by Michel Fehr, Ramona Naddaff, and Nadia Tazi, 86–127. New York: Zone Books.

Magliocco, Sabina. 1993. *The Two Madonnas: The Politics of Festival in a Sardinian Community.* New York: Peter Lang.

Manning, Frank E. 1989. "Carnival in Canada: The Politics of Celebration." In *Folk Groups and Folklore Genres: A Reader*, edited by Elliot Oring, 78–87. Logan: Utah State University Press.

Manuel, Peter. 1988. *Popular Musics of the Non-Western World*. New York: Oxford University Press.

Mariani, John. 1998. "Arrivederci Roma!" In *American Way*, vol. 31, no. 24: 42–7.

Mazzonis, Fillipo. 1994. "Abruzzo: Un modello vincente con due nei, clientelismo e provincialismo." In *Stato dell'Italia*, edited by Paul Ginsborg, 182–6. Milano: Bruno Mondadori.

Mauss, Marcel. 1973 [1936]. "Techniques of the Body." In *Economy and Society*, vol. 2, no. 1: 70–88.

McCarl, Robert S. 1985. *The District of Columbia Fire Fighters' Project: A Case Study in Occupational Folklife*. Washington, DC: Smithsonian Institution.

Mead, Margaret. 1935. *Sex and Temperament in Three Primitive Societies*. New York: Morrow.

Mechling, Jay. 1996. "Folklore and the Mass Media." In *American Folklore: An Encyclopedia*, edited by Jan Harold Brunvand, 462–3. New York: Garland Publishing, Inc.

Merleau-Ponty, Maurice. 1981. *Phenomenology of Perception.* Translated by Colin Smith. London: Routledge and Kegan Paul.

Mutti, Antonio. 1994. "Il particolarismo come risorsa. Politica ed economia nello sviluppo Abruzzese." In *Rassegna Italiana di sociologia*, vol. 4, Dicembre: 451–519.

Narayan, Kirin. 1992. "Refractions of the Field at Home: American Representations of Hindu Holy Men in the 19th and 20th Centuries." In *Cultural Anthropology*, vol. 8, no. 4: 476–509.

Nardini, Gloria. 1999. *Che Bella Figura!: The Power of Performance in an Italian Ladies' Club in Chicago.* Albany: State University of New York Press.

Neils, Kathleen Conzen, David A. Gerber, Ewa Morawska, George Possets, and Rudolph J. Vecoli. 1990. "The Invention of Ethnicity: A Perspective from the USA." In *Journal of American Ethnic History*, vol. 12, no 1: 3–41.

Noyes, Dorothy. 1995. "Facade Performances: Public Face, Private Mask." In *Southern Folklore*, vol. 52, no. 2: 91–7.

– 1998. "*La maja vestida*: Dress as Resistance to Enlightment in Late-18th-Century Madrid." In *Journal of American Folklore*, vol. 111, no. 440: 197–217.

Paredes, Américo. 1958. *With His Pistol in His Hand: A Border Ballad and Its Hero.* Austin: University of Texas Press.

Parmentier, Richard J. 1993. "The Political Function of Reported Speech: A Belauan Example." In *Reflexive Language*, edited by John A. Lucy, 261–86. Cambridge: Cambridge University Press.

Parsons, Talcott. 1951. *The Social System.* Glencoe, IL: Free Press.

Passarelli, Pasquale. 1998. *Abruzzo.* Acquaviva d'Isernia: Isituto Enciclopedico Italiano.

Peristiany, John. 1966. *Honour and Shame: The Values of Mediterranean Society.* Chicago: University of Chicago Press.

Pieterse, Jan Nederveeen. 1995. "Globalization as Hybridization." In *Global Modernities*, edited by Mike Featherstone et al., 45–68. London: Sage Publications.

Pitkin, Donald S. 1993. "Italian Urbanscape: Intersection of Private and Public." In *The Cultural Meaning of Urban Space*, edited by Robert Rotenberg and Gary McDonough, 95–101. Westport, CT: Bergin and Garvey.

Pitrè, Giuseppe. 1913. *La famiglia, la casa, la vita del popolo Siciliano.* Palermo: Reber.

Pocius, Gerald L. 1991. *A Place to Belong: Community Order and Everyday Space in Calvert, Newfoundland.* Athens: University of Georgia Press.

Polhemus, Ted. 1994. *Streetstyle: From Sidewalk to Catwalk.* New York: Thames and Hudson.

Pred, Allan and Michael John Watts. 1992. *Reworking Modernity: Capitalisms and Symbolic Discontent.* New Brunswick, NJ: Rutgers University Press.

Radner, Joan N. and Susan S. Lanser. 1987. "The Feminist Voice: Strategies of Coding in Folklore and Literature." In *Journal of American Folklore*, vol. 100, no. 398: 412–25.

Radway, Janice. 1984. *Reading the Romance: Women, Patriarchy, and Popular Literature*. Chapel Hill: University of North Carolina Press.

Reed-Danahay, Deborah E. 1997. *Auto/ethnography: Rewriting the Self and the Social*. Oxford: Berg.

Robertson, Roland. 1995. "Glocalization: Time-Space and Homogeneity-Heterogeneity." In *Global Modernities*, edited by Mike Featherstone et al., 23–44. London: Sage Publications.

Romanucci-Ross, Lola. 1991. *One Hundred Towers: An Italian Odyssey of Cultural Survival*. New York: Bergin and Garvey.

Rostow, W.W. 1960. *The Stages of Economic Growth*. Cambridge: Cambridge University Press.

Rutter, Derek R. 1984. *Looking and Seeing: The Role of Visual Communication in Social Interaction*. Toronto: Wiley.

Saunders, George R. 1984. "Contemporary Italian Cultural Anthropology." In *American Review of Anthropology*, vol. 13, October: 447–66.

Sawin, Patricia E. 2002. "Performance at the Nexus of Gender, Power, and Desire: Reconsidering Bauman's *Verbal Art* from the Perspective of Gendered Subjectivity as Performance." In *Journal of American Folklore*, vol. 115, no. 455: 28–61.

Schiller, H.I. 1985. "Electronic Information Flows: New Basis for Global Domination?" In *Television in Transition*, edited by P. Drummond and R. Patterson, 11–20. London: British Film Institute.

Scobey, David. 1992. "Anatomy of the Promenade: The Politics of Bourgeois Sociability in Nineteenth-Century New York." In *Social History*, vol. 17, no. 2: 203–27.

Severgnini, Beppe. 2002. *Ciao, America!: An Italian Discovers the U.S.* New York: Broadway Books.

Shostak, Marjorie. 1981. *Nisa: The Life and Words of a!Kung Woman*. New York: Vintage Books.

Silverman, Sydel. 1975. *Three Bells of Civilization*. New York: Columbia University Press.

Singer, Milton B. 1972. *When a Great Tradition Modernizes: An Anthropological Approach to Indian Civilization*. New York: Praeger Publishers.

Smith, Dorothy E. 1997. *The Everyday World as Problematic: A Feminist Sociology*. Boston: Northeastern University Press.

Sollors, Werner. 1986. *Beyond Ethnicity: Consent and Descent in American Culture*. New York: Oxford University Press.

Solomon, Thomas. 1994. "*Coplas de Todos Santos* in Cochambamba: Language, Music, and Performance in Bolivian Quecha Song Dueling." In *Journal of American Folklore*, vol. 107, no. 425: 378–414.

Stahl, Sandra K.D. 1989. *Literary Folkloristics and the Personal Narrative*. Bloomington: Indiana University Press.

Stern, Stephen and John Allan Cicala, eds. 1991. *Creative Ethnicity: Symbols and Strategies of Contemporary Ethnic Life*. Logan: Utah State University Press.

Stoeltje, Beverly J. 1988. "Introduction: Feminist Revisions in Folklore Studies." In *Journal of Folklore Research*, vol. 25, no. 3: 141–53.

– 1992. "Festival." In *Folklore, Cultural Performances, and Popular Entertainments*, edited by Richard Bauman, 261–72. Oxford: Oxford University Press.

Stoeltje, Beverly J. and Richard Bauman. 1989. "Community Festival and the Enactment of Modernity." In *The Old Traditional Way of Life*, edited by Robert Walls and George Shoemaker, 159–71. Bloomington: Trickster Press.

Stone, Ruth and Verlon L. Stone. 1981. "Event, Feedback, and Analysis: Research Media in the Study of Music Events." In *Ethnomusicology*, vol. 25, no. 2: 215–25.

Strathern, Marilyn. 1987. "The Limits of Auto-ethnography." In *Anthropology at Home*, edited by Anthony Jackson, 16–37. London: Tavistock.

Sullenberger, Tom E. 1974. "Ajax Meets the Jolly Green Giant: Some Observations on the Use of Folklore in the American Mass Media." In *Journal of American Folklore*, vol. 87, no. 343: 53–85.

Synott, Anthony and David Howes. 1992. "From Measurement to Meaning: Anthropologies of the Body." In *Anthropologia*, vol. 87, no. 1–3: 147–66.

Taylor, Charles. 1999. "Two Theories of Modernity." In *Public Culture*, vol. 11, no. 1: 153–75.

Thoms, William. 1964. "Folklore." In *The Study of Folklore*, edited by Alan Dundes, 4–6. Englewood Cliffs, NJ: Prentice Hall, Inc.

Toelken, Barre. 1979. *The Dynamics of Folklore*. Boston: Houghton Miflin Company.

Tomalison, John. 1991. *Cultural Imperialism: A Critical Introduction*. London: Pinter.

Tönnies, Ferdinand. 1963. *Community & Society*. Translated and edited by Charles P. Loomis. New York: Harper & Row.

Tricarico, Donald. 1991. "Guido: Fashioning an Italian-American Youth Style." In *Journal of Ethnic Studies*, vol. 19, no. 1: 41–66.

Triolo, Nancy. 1993. "Mediterranean Exotica and the Mafia 'Other,' or Problems of Representation in Pitrè's Texts." In *Cultural Anthropology*, vol. 8, no. 3: 306–16.

Turner, Victor. 1969. *The Ritual Process*. Chicago: Aldine.

Turone, Sergio. 1993. *Agonia di un regime: Il caso Abruzzo*. Rome: Laterza.

Vidich, Arthur J. and Joseph Bensman. 1968. *Small Town in Mass Society: Class, Power, and Religion in a Rural Community*. Princeton: Princeton University Press.

Vigarello, Georges. 1988. *Concepts of Cleanliness: Changing Attitudes in France since the Middle Ages*. Translated by Jean Birrell. Cambridge: Cambridge University Press.

– 1989. "The Upward Training of the Body from the Age of Chivalry to Courtly Civility." In *Fragments of a History of the Human Body, Part II*, edited by Michel Fehr, Ramona Naddaff, and Nadia Tazi, 148–99. New York: Zone Books.

Visconti, Andrea. 1994. "Alexander in carcere." In *Il Centro* 2 February 1994: 7.

Watts, Michael John. 1992. "Capitalisms, Crises, and Culture I: Notes Toward a Totality of Fragments." In *Reworking Modernity: Capitalisms and Symbolic Discontent*, 1–20. New Brunswick, NJ: Rutgers University Press.

Webb, Michael. 1990. *The City Square: A Historical Evolution*. New York: Whitney Library of Design, Watson-Guptill Publications.

Weber, Max. 1968. *Economy and Society: An Outline of Interpretive Sociology*, edited by Gunther Roth and Claus Wittich. New York: Bedminster Press.

Weinstein, Deena. 1991. *Heavy Metal: A Cultural Sociology*. New York: Lexington Books.

Willis, Paul. 1975. "The Expressive Style of Motor Bike Culture." In *The Body as a Medium of Expression*, edited by Jonathan Benthal and Ted Polhemus, 233–52. London: Allen Lane.

– 1977. *Learning to Labour: How Working Class Kids Get Working Class Jobs*. Farnborough: Saxon House.

Wilson, Kathryn E. 1996. "Folk Costume." In *American Folklore: An Encyclopedia*, edited by Jan Harold Brunvand, 161–4. New York: Garland Publishing, Inc.

Witrock, Bjorn. 2000. "Modernity: One, None, or Many? European Origins and Modernity as a Global Condition." In *Daedalus*, vol. 129, no. 1: 31–61.

Wolff, Janet. 1997. "The Global and the Specific: Reconciling Conflicting Theories of Culture." In *Culture, Globalization, and the World-System: Contemporary Conditions for the Representation of Identity*, edited by Anthony King, 161–74. Minneapolis: University of Minnesota Press.

Yoder, Don. 1963. "The Folklife Studies Movement." In *Pennsylvania Folklife*, vol. 13, no. 3: 43–56.

– 1972. "Folk Costume." In *Folklore and Folklife: An Introduction*, edited by Richard M. Dorson, 295–324. Chicago: University of Chicago Press.

Young, Iris Marion. 1990. "Throwing Like a Girl." In *Throwing Like a Girl and Other Essays in Feminist Philosophy and Social Theory*, 140–59. Bloomington: Indiana University Press.

Young, Katharine. 1994. "Whose Body? An Introduction to Bodylore." In *Journal of American Folklore*, vol. 107, no. 423: 3–8.

Zucher, Paul. 1959. *Town and Square*. Cambridge: MIT Press.

Index